Actors! Sto

A Comprehensive Guide to Building Income Streams That Allow You To Pursue Your Artistic Passions

Copyright © Alex Witherow 2019

Introduction

The past few years, actors and artists regularly ask me to coffee to pick my brain about the issues they're having with their side jobs. The conversation goes something like this: "My side job is killing me. I'm so drained from it. I may just quit acting altogether and get a stable job." The profile of these people is usually 30-something actors who have been in the industry since their early 20s. They most likely have a BFA or MFA or they've trained in high level studios for many years. They've had a handful of notable acting jobs. Probably a few TV or stage credits that would look impressive. They have a decent agent—not a CAA, ICM, or Gersh-type agency, but mid-level agent—who is getting them in front of the right producers and casting directors. While things are moving along decently, they are exhausted. Their acting career is progressing at a snail's pace and they're tired of being poor. Have you ever noticed you don't know many actors in their 40s or 50s? It's like they all vanish. I can count all the ones I know on one hand. Where have they gone? Most likely, they're tired of snail-pace progress and being poor and have given up on their dream.

Many times we are conditioned to think, as actors, that we are one big gig away from never having to wait tables, or do anything else other than act, again. While those big breaks do exist, the probability of you ONLY relying on acting income for the next 10 to 15 years or more is low. Think about when you watch the Golden Globes or the Oscars. You seem to be watching the same 200 stars who are undoubtedly rich. But what about the rest of us? Many are living off of acting income, but it's a very paycheck-to-paycheck situation and certainly not steady. I want to help you diversify your income streams so that you have options when it comes to how you make your salary.

What would happen if you took the 30 hours a week of being at a survival job and devoted that to your artistic career in terms of training, networking, and/or developing content for yourself? What if you did that for a month, a year, 5 years? Do you realize how much faster your career would progress gaining all that time back? Your survival job is setting you back 10 years on breaking out in your acting or artistic career.

This book is designed to not only help you get out of the starving-artist mentality but, most importantly, to get your checking account out of that place as well. We have a unique challenge as actors. We must make a maximum amount of money in our survival job in a minimum amount of time so that we can focus on our creative careers. We need total flexibility—time to audition, take classes, write, and network and whatever else needs to be done to progress our careers. We also need money for headshots, classes, mailings, clothing, makeup, having your hair done, etc. It's expensive being an actor or artist! It's also nice to go on a vacation every now and then too!

Why listen to me? In the words of Liam Neeson, "I have a very particular set of skills" and it makes me specially qualified to talk on this topic. I'm also living a maximum-income-on-minimum-time-spent lifestyle. I'm in my late 30s and have been in the industry for 13 years. My resume is very similar to what I described above, but let me tell you something, I DO NOT like being poor. You probably don't either. In my undergrad years, I studied at a top-5 entrepreneurship program in the country and then trained to be an actor after university. I'm as skilled at starting a company as I am at acting. I also worked in sales for many years in my 20s, including at the top software sales organization in the world, so I am well versed in tech and business development. I consider myself a perfect hybrid of artist and entrepreneur. But you don't have to be a business genius to make an extra $2,000-$5,000 per month or more. It is completely attainable, and I want to show you how.

If you're a younger actor in your 20s, I'm talking to you too. You may think right now, "Hey, I don't mind waiting tables! It's an actor rite of passage! I can live off of $2,000 per month no problem!" I implore you to keep reading. There is a ticking time bomb inside of you. It's called "your tolerance for poverty." It is quietly decreasing each and every year. It will not last forever. You will hit a wall with having roommates eventually. You may have to support a spouse or a child at some point. I want to give you strategies to think ahead before this time-bomb goes off in your head and you throw in the towel on your creative career. Now is the time to build good monetary habits.

Keep an open mind as you read. I guarantee the way I think about money is very foreign to the way you think about money. I'm typing this right now on the way to a vacation in the British West Indies. I'm also getting paid at the same time. I don't say that to brag; I say it because I want you to have the same freedom. I want you to be making maximum money with minimal time spent, to give you options when it comes to building a great artistic career and a great life. It is possible! Let's get started.

Dedication

For every actor or artist who has come to me asking for advice who feels like he or she is drowning financially in the artistic lifestyle. I hear your despair regularly, and with the utmost empathy for you, I want to give you the tools to get unstuck as best as I can. You all have beautiful gifts and hearts as artists, whether it be as an actor, writer, singer, director, painter, or anything else. But for many of you, that flame has been extinguished because you've gotten tired of being poor. This book is for you.

Table of Contents

Introduction

Dedication

Chapter 1 - The Art of the Survival Job: An Overview

Chapter 2 - Bars and Restaurants No More: Defining the Perfect Income Situation

Chapter 3 - Options, Options, Options: The Different Types of Income

Chapter 4 - Getting Down to Brass Tacks: The Process of Finding Your Own Income

Chapter 5 - Not Just For A*sholes: How To Think Like An Entrepreneur

Chapter 6 - What To Do With All Your Free Time Now? Career Gains

Chapter 7 - I Know You're Whining: Responding To Your Objections and Resistance

Chapter 8 - Thinking About Quitting the Artistic Lifestyle? What It's Like On the Other Side

Chapter 9 - My Story As An Artist and Entrepreneur

Chapter 10 - You Can Do This! My Final Benediction

Appendix - Sample Contract For Connector Deals

Chapter 1 - The Art of the Survival Job: An Overview

"If you don't learn how to make money while you sleep, you'll work until you die." –Warren Buffett

Let's be honest, acting pay can be consistent, but most of the time it is not. How do we deal with this inconsistency? I have a friend who worked on Spike Lee's new *She's Gotta Have It* and made a nice check from being on seasons 1 and 2. She probably made around $10-15K if my calculations are right based on the SAG scale on Netflix. To many of you, you may think, "Holy shit! I'd be rich with that in the bank." I'm sorry to inform you, $15K will not last long, especially in Manhattan or LA. You need to start thinking about diversifying your income streams—acting is only one of them.

I heard an interview from Seth Rogen once and he basically said, "Being an actor is ultimately a war of attrition. You have to outlast everyone else." He's dead right. Your mindset shouldn't be about getting that big break, it should be about not giving up. The break comes when it's ready to come, after many years of improving your craft, your mind, your network, and with alignment with your "type" in the industry. But as I mentioned in the introduction, time and your tolerance for poverty are working against you. And look, you may be cool with living in a studio in Manhattan until you die, but I don't want that for you, and I assume you don't want that either if you're reading this book. Additionally, there is a supply glut of actors that are in their 20s (when everyone's fresh-faced and optimistic). Each subsequent decade, the numbers drop exponentially. Your competition by the time you're 45 or 55 is a fraction of what it was in your 20s, as Seth intimated. You must be built to last.

Much of our problem with our thinking is no one taught us how to make money. Our education system focuses on algebra, geometry, humanities, etc. Those are all wonderful things, but they don't put a meal on your table much of the time—they aren't transferable skills. If you're like me, you were brought up by two parents who had stable jobs—my dad worked at the same company for 30 years and my mom was a teacher her whole career. Those are honorable life courses, but I was bequeathed the mentality of "one job, one income." If you lose your job, you are screwed. In 2019, this is absolutely the wrong mentality! We are getting out of this thinking moving forward.

As time ticks by, we get more and more tired of living paycheck to paycheck. Your tolerance of poverty dwindles by the year. I know people living with roommates at age 43—they are not into it, trust me. Your parents may be cool with paying your bills at age 25, but it gets real old for them by 35. Many times we secretly think, "Someone will save me. I'll marry someone rich who will give me a stable life." And yes, I think we all know a few actors or actresses where that has happened, but most of us are not going to be sponsored actors, and you shouldn't desire to be. You will respect yourself so much more when you are self-sustaining. And aside from that, if you talk to those actors who have wealthy spouses, there are always strings attached. It's not as glamorous as it looks from the outside.

I once had a conversation with Sam Rockwell's acting coach, who said, "Acting has to be all that you can do. When your back is against the wall, that's when you make it." I understand what he was saying, but I disagree on some level. What punches you through is your passion, your skill level, your network, and the marketability of your type. All four have to be at a max level. You're not going to accomplish that on 5 hours a week devoted to your career and a waiter's salary. You must have more time and money at your disposal.

Our acting career is a business and it needs funding. Another time, I had a conversation with Leo DiCaprio's acting coach, who stated, "All acting problems are either a craft problem or a psychological problem. You have to invest in both." He is 100% correct. In business we have what is called product development. To truly maximize profits, your product has to be superior. As an actor, you are the product. I know that sounds crass when you have an artist's mentality, but trust me, producers and agents definitely see you this way. Creating an optimal product is about investing in your training (which you should consider ongoing) and unwinding the knots in your mind, which can include going to therapy (this also is ongoing many times). And if you've done training or therapy, you know it's not cheap. I would add to this that you need *time* to network as well as create content for yourself, which is why we need flexibility in our schedules. If you're waiting around for your agent to pass the perfect script along that fits you like a glove, you might be waiting years. It's better to just go out there and write it for yourself. We're seeing this more and more with different stars in Hollywood. They're all creating their own production companies and their own content that fits them. They also have the luxury of doing this because they have enough money to fund the company and to take time off to write for themselves in between movies. You need the same luxury to propel yourself.

The goal of this book is to give you the tools to learn how to create multiple income streams, thus allowing you time to develop your "product." The ultimate goal is becoming a full-time actor, but still making money on the side that can sustain you even when you have dry spells in your creative career. The 30 hours a week you're losing on a side job is killing your career, and you need those hours back. It's time to really start valuing your time! We are going to get into a mindset of making many more dollars per hour than what is offered at the local restaurant and doing so in a less taxing way on the body. In my own life, I am an absolute stickler with my time—I value it so much. My goal for you is to reduce your weekly commitment on side jobs to 4-5 hours per week, tops. You can do it, I promise.

Chapter 2 - Bars and Restaurants No More: Defining the Perfect Income Situation

When P90X came out, they marketed themselves to fitness junkies and beginners as a workout program that creates "functional strength." What did that mean? It meant that you would do workouts to their videos, but it wouldn't make you huge and muscular. You built functional strength to make you strong in your day-to-day activities, but there wasn't an excess of strength like you would see with a body builder. If you see people who have done P90X, they're usually very defined and cut but never huge or overly muscular. In the same way, I want you to learn to develop *functional income*—a comfortable lifestyle that you can live off of but that still gives you a good chunk of time each week to work on your career or any artistic endeavors. We're valuing time over money but still making adequate money.

I'll keep it simple for you: the perfect income situation is maximum money on minimal time spent. You should be able to live off your income streams on 4-5 hours of work per week. Aside from that, we need total flexibility. If you get a call for an audition, you have to go and prepare. We don't deal with bosses, managers, shift captains, and restaurant owners anymore. You are the boss, so you make the call on how your schedule is set. This is key to our situation, and you should not accept anything less than what I've just outlined. Also, ideally, you don't want to take your work home with you mentally, but that is sometimes hard to achieve when you're an entrepreneur. It is an added bonus if you can achieve mental freedom.

That said, what is tricky about being a functional income entrepreneur is that many of these people build great businesses but work very HARD, 60-80 hours a week or more. Often they become very wealthy because they've scaled their business model many times over. We obviously can't do this as artists/functional-income entrepreneurs. Our goal is to SUSTAIN ourselves comfortably while we pursue our dreams as actors or artists. This is why you can't work a 9-5 job in most cases. You're losing too much time and you're under someone else's thumb for a 1/3 of your life. More on that later; I have plenty of experience with it!

If we think of this in the form of a continuum, on the far left, we have someone trading their time for money at a minimal rate. On the opposite end of the spectrum, we have a full-time entrepreneur in a successful business who is making big money but also spending a ton of time on the business. Neither end of the spectrum works for the actor or artist. We must master the middle of the continuum, where we have a high-dollar-per-hour skill and passive income opportunities but spend minimal time.

Building The Dream
When it comes to what we want to accomplish, I usually advise people to start small. Don't quit your shitty survival job yet, but let's focus on how to build this. In the first three months, you should be able to build a side gig that brings in $2,000 per month. Ultimately, the ideal situation is to have 3-4 different income streams that generate $2,000 a month and are scalable. Once you have those set up, you can expand each one to grow —sometimes side gigs are scalable, sometimes they're not. Obviously it's better if they are, but it's not the end of the world if they're not. We're not going to turn away an easy $2,000 a month.

The key thing here is to get OFF the service level and into the management/delegation level. What is the service level? Waiter, caterer, being someone else's b*tch in any form, etc. That's not good for your finances and it's definitely not good for your mindset as an actor or artist. If you're going into auditions being yelled at regularly and treated like a servant, that is terrible for your confidence. As we know, confidence is key when it comes to booking roles or just doing anything effectively in life. Aside from that, service work is tough on your body.

I know what you're thinking: "Yeah, sure, an extra $2,000 a month would be amazing, but how the hell do I do that? I don't have any money to start a business." What we're going to do here is build one income stream, then a second, then a third, and so on. The goal is to ween yourself off of the shitty side job so that you never have to work for Chad, the douche canoe shift captain, ever again. It's all about baby steps and starting small.

Valuing Time Over Money
I've alluded to this already, but we're going to get hyper-vigilant about valuing our time. Later on I will discuss the levels of scaling a functional income stream, but in the meantime, we have to learn the fundamentals. When you work for someone else, you will always make minimal dollars per hour. When you work for yourself, you will make way more money per hour, period. We are going to develop a high-dollar-per-hour skill that you most likely already have, focus on expanding on that income stream, and then add passive income opportunities around it. This formula will give you a comfortable lifestyle as a functional income entrepreneur and allow you many hours a week to focus on your artistic endeavors. Our goal isn't to work for someone else, which consumes our week for minimal money, nor start a company that also consumes our week for maximum money. We're going to inhabit the sweet spot in the middle of that continuum as actors and artists. Maximum money, minimum time.

How Should We View Money?
This is an interesting question, because after reading thus far, you may think, "Geez, this guy is obsessed with making money! I don't know if I identify with this mindset at all." Don't get me wrong—I love making money! But I think there is an important distinction to be made here. I see money as something that we should control and not let control us. Grant Cardone, famous real estate entrepreneur, always says, "Get your money to work as hard for you as you work for it." This is the key. You can be smart about making money and pursuing your dreams and, at the same time, not be *controlled* by money. Money isn't the root of all evil, but having an unhealthy love and obsession with it is. The end goal isn't to acquire money. My feeling is that if you have a functional income with the option to expand those income streams, you will be putting yourself in position to really have a rewarding life. You'll be able to pursue your artistic passions but also not have your back against the wall with your side job. That is really important. You will be controlling the things you want to pursue *as well as* how you sustain yourself.

Chapter 3 - Options, Options, Options: The Different Types of Income

This is my favorite thing to talk about, because now we get into the nitty gritty of the options for you. I will say this: what your income streams look like will be different than your friend's income streams, which will be different from someone else. We all have different talents and interests, but there are some guidelines I think that are best to follow. Let's discuss the different types of incomes and their pros and cons.

Service jobs - high dollar per hour versus low dollar per hour
Before, I said get off the service level. And you should, assuming it's paying under $35 per hour. Your body and eventually your mind won't allow you to wait tables, cater, or bartend forever. If you're doing bottle service, I think we can both agree that's not going to last, albeit being very lucrative. Your body will reach a point where working on your feet for 8 to 10 hours per shift just will not happen anymore. It's tiring work. Just a hint: that point comes around age 35.

Let's say you are a private chef and you're cooking for high-end clientele at $500 or more per meal on a Thursday or Friday night. This is an example of a high-dollar-per-hour service job. This is a great thing! If you are a private chef, I would assume you love cooking and are very skilled at it. Plus, in this scenario, you're servicing clients as opposed to taking barking orders from Chad. There is a significant difference in how you're treated in this scenario, and therefore, it is much less psychologically taxing. High-dollar-per-hour service jobs that are $50-$100+ per hour are great to have and are usually flexible to some degree. I guarantee you have some type of skill set that can garner this kind of money—especially if you're college educated.

The key to high-dollar-per-hour jobs is that they must be sustainable. Working in bottle service is not sustainable, being a private chef is. We want to make you built to last. Here are a few examples of good jobs in this category: private chef, business/marketing consultant, nutritionist, therapist, lawyer, line producer, script doctor, film editor, personal trainer, event planner, online ad manager, copywriter, voiceover artist, social media manager, commodities trader, property manager, acting coach, life coach, etc.

As we move forward, think of a high-dollar-per-hour skill you may already have. If you don't have one, we are going to address how to figure this out later in the book. You may also have another skill that I didn't list. Hang onto that in your mind for now.

Selling Access to Assets
The most notorious form of selling access to assets is Airbnb, but there are other as well. This form of income is about selling access of your assets for others to borrow or rent (e.g., houses, apartments, cars, event spaces, boats, etc. What's great about this form of income is that it takes very little work and yields a great hourly rate.

I milk this form of income to its max because I love it so much. I rent apartments and Airbnb them. I Airbnb my own apartment when I'm gone. I have multiple cars that I rent to Uber drivers full-time. I have an event space in my building that I rent out on occasion. I also rent out my yacht to Instagram models for photo shoots (kidding, kidding). However, this is a fantastic way to make passive income. For the last 4 years I've had at least one extra apartment that I Airbnb full-time and it pays for the rent on my personal apartment. It takes about 1-2 hours a week of upkeep, if that.

1. Apartments and Airbnb
I had an actor talk to me once about his two-bedroom apartment and how his roommate was moving out. I told him "DO NOT GET A NEW ROOMMATE, Airbnb the room." His first response was "will I get enough bookings to cover the rent?" Yes, you will, and you will pay for your own rent as well unless you live in the middle of nowhere. But if you're near Manhattan or LA or a major city, which I assume you are, you will be fine. I've known friends who Airbnb'd apartments all the way up in Washington Heights—a 40 min train ride to Times Square—and they had bookings year round. I also know people in Jersey City, Hoboken, Williamsburg, Bushwick, way out in Brooklyn, Hollywood, East Los Angeles, Santa Monica, Long Beach, etc. that have had bookings year round as well. The demand to get into major markets is like drinking from a fire hose. Hotel prices in Manhattan start at $250 per night, so a $150/night or less Airbnb is a very attractive option to travelers.

House owners across the country do this regularly. They buy houses and Airbnb them to not only pay their mortgage but make a $2,000+ profit each month. That said, there has been legislation in different cities outlawing Airbnb. The reason why is because hotel lobbies of different cities are fighting against Airbnb since it's majorly cutting into their profits. In Manhattan, the hotel lobby is basically a cartel. They've all colluded together to create a price floor at $250 per night. Unfortunately, they have enough money and clout to pressure the city and state government and have gotten Airbnb outlawed for the most part. They cloak it under the guise of "keeping unruly guests out of neighborhoods," but it's really about money.

If you live in Manhattan or nearby within New York state, the new law as of 2019 prohibits having an entire apartment used for Airbnb. That said, if you live in the apartment and are Airbnbing a room within your apartment, that is legal (so long as you're present). In New Jersey, they're a lot looser on all of this, which has been my solution. That said, the hotel lobby on the other side of the Hudson river has even started challenging Airbnb in city municipalities. Even while I was living in the East Village, I Airbnb'd an apartment in Hoboken for a year. I've heard in LA, there has been a similar crackdown specifically in Santa Monica, but in other parts like Hollywood or East LA, you can Airbnb as much as you want. Definitely get the scoop on your area should you decide to do this, but I can guarantee that just having a spare room to Airbnb will be fine no matter where you are.

I will speak more on potential objections and the nitty gritty details of Airbnb in later chapters—it's not always roses and cash, but overall, it's been great. If you're seriously contemplating this option for income (and you should), you want to do your research on the laws of your neighborhood, check out hosting message boards, etc. Get the full scoop on your area. And as always, a sure bet for not having any issues with a landlord is to find a private owner who is renting his or her apartment and ask if you have permission to Airbnb.

2. Cars
Believe it or not, you can loan your cars to others for a daily rate as well. There are a few sites that do this, namely Turo, Getaround, and Hyrecar. This is a relatively new thing in the market but fairly scalable and easier to get into than renting or owning an apartment. As of the publishing of this e-book, I have a small fleet of four cars that I rent mainly to full-time Uber

drivers for an increased rate per week because they're using it for their own income.

I got into this because I was an Uber driver for a year about 4 years ago and saw that there were car leasing companies for drivers in Long Island City. I remember when I saw that I thought, "That's a lot easier to handle than driving 30 hours a week!" That said, running this type of operation in one of the five boroughs would require you to have a TLC (Taxi and Limousine Commission) base license, which is costly. Like Airbnb, I moved this operation over to New Jersey, where the regulations are much easier. I didn't have to deal with New York City or NY state taxi leasing company requirements.

While there was a learning curve to this business—mainly figuring out how to source quality drivers—it became a very stable source of income for me 4 months after starting. And it requires under an hour of work per week, easily. I rent the cars to drivers after screening them, and they pay weekly rent on it. Yes, I've had some bad apples and had to take the car back, and I budget about $300/month for repairs and oil changes for the drivers, but other than that, it's been a smooth source of income.

Getting into the car game typically requires good credit and about $0 to $500 down to finance or lease a car. If you like the hands off approach, I recommend GetAround. They will literally take your car, install a GPS tracking and remote access device on it and manage your bookings for you. They split bookings 60/40 with car owners so you make about $45 a day on the car in revenue. All you really need to take care of are car washes and repairs on occasion. The GetAround option isn't as profitable as the way I run my business, but it is VERY hands off and has many fewer headaches. You'll make easily $500 to $800 a month per car in profit after all your car expenses are paid and never have to deal with any parking tickets, toll violations, etc. It's a pretty good deal.

3. Event Spaces
Do you have a sick backyard in LA or Brooklyn or a fancy loft that Chad the douche canoe shift captain would love to invite all his influencer friends to for a cocktail party? Do you have access to a space someone could use for business meetings or a conference? There is a site called Splacer that is essentially Airbnb for event spaces. My building has a nice cocktail area and you guessed it, I have it up on Splacer!

The traffic on Splacer's site isn't quite as strong as Airbnb, but I get bookings on it every now and then. Every time I get a booking it's easily $500-$1000 for a few hours of hosting at your apartment, house, or event space. That's money you didn't have before, for minimal work!

As you can see, selling access to assets is a great way to go for an artist's lifestyle. There are a lot of different ways you can milk money from different assets for minimal time spent, and I recommend you do so. I almost exclusively live off of this form of income.

Selling Knowledge, Experience, and/or Intellectual Property
This genre of income would be like what I'm doing with writing a book—selling knowledge and my experiences. Another form of this would be the TV script I wrote that I'm in the process of selling.

We all have unique experiences, ideas, knowledge, etc. That said, the internet has made these assets much more accessible to monetize. For example, in the old days, you wrote a book that was 40,000 to 60,000 words and you had to shop it to a publisher. The process would take years, and even if your book was published, profits weren't guaranteed to be that high. The time and effort for the reward was barely worth it. Now, with self-publishing sites like Amazon and others, reaching the public directly is very attainable, with minimal cost.

The key to driving sales with an e-book is having a following online. For as much as people tease social-media influencers, they have large audiences and can drive a lot of traffic to certain products. Online sales is mainly just a numbers game and having a good marketing hook. X amount of impressions turn into Y amount of conversations and Z sales.

Many of you are pros with social media and driving followers, especially in LA. Many times, as actors, we think we need followers to show agents/casting directors/producers/directors that we're relevant online and that's why you should cast us! Like me, you've probably heard a story from a casting director where it came down to two actors for a role and they went with the person who had a larger online following. Because of this, many of us have spent a lot of time growing an online presence. Why not use that following to drive sales for a product?

Some of you may be thinking, "What would I write about? I have nothing to say in a book." I think your voice will emerge over time naturally if you observe the conversations you have with people and notice your own passions as well. It's been very clear for me. I spent most of my 20s in the business and entrepreneurial worlds, so when I got back into the performance world in my late 20s, I saw things from a very different perspective than most actors. Like Seth Rogen pointed out, I knew that longevity as an actor had much to do with winning the war of attrition. And to do that, one had to escape being exasperated by poverty. And fortunately for me, I was literally trained in undergrad with regards to how to turn nothing into something monetarily, so here I am talking to you.

I've noticed that actors are always interested in talking about their survival job and how they sustain themselves. People are constantly trying to figure that out. I get asked about my situation a lot because people know I came from the business world. I've been encouraged repeatedly to write a book about it, so here I am. I say this to point out that eventually, your voice and passion becomes clear.

Some of you may have zero interest in writing non-fiction. You may be all about writing fictional scripts. I consider myself in that camp as well on some level. I think writing is cathartic and a great way to create opportunities for yourself in your career, even if you don't sell your script or self-produce it. Much of selling a script is about creating a compelling story that is germane to the zeitgeist of our modern society but also knowing the right people to get in front of. More on that later in my networking chapter.

Connector deals and brokering (selling access to your network)
When I say brokering, am I talking about real estate? I mean, yes, that is a form of brokering. Brokering is being the middle man in any business transaction. Your agent is a broker. Your agent vets talent and brings the appropriate people to casting directors, producers, directors, etc., because those people are too busy to find their own talent, basically, and they want someone to vouch for you. The internet has killed many brokering professions because it serves as a giant broker. This is a good thing by the way. You used to have to call a travel agent to book a trip or a flight, but an extra fee was added on to your trip. Ever used a broker to get an apartment in Manhattan and paid the fee? Yeah, F*$% that. Technology should eradicate the need for talent agents eventually, but our industry is very slow moving when it comes to technology adoption.

So what do I mean when I say *connector* deals? Let me tell you two stories—one about a writer friend of mine and another about me. One of us did the deal right and the other did it wrong. We'll start with the one that went wrong.

My friend is good friends with a famous pop singer and that singer's spiritual advisor. Using his strong entrepreneurial and creative mind, along with a great network, he had a superb idea. He thought, "What if we pitch a documentary to Netflix about the spiritual journey of this famous pop singer that has already been very public. The documentary would interview both the singer and the spiritual advisor on the details of this journey." First off, I love the idea and the concept, but the devil is always in the details. He called up his friends at Netflix and pitched this idea. They loved it. Everything is going swimmingly at this point. The only problem is that, many times, us creative folk struggle with the legal elements of business transactions (I've definitely been guilty of this). He was over at my pool a month later telling me about this deal, and it was looking like this documentary could push through. I asked him, "Are you getting a cut of this since you're brokering this deal?" The problem was that he was doing all this work to get this deal done, but had no way of getting paid and had nothing in writing. Netflix was going to take the idea and run with it, leaving him with nothing.

This is a great example of a well-done and creative connector deal, but you have to get paid too for your time and work! How do we ensure payment? When I went through sales training at the top corporate program in the world, they drilled us with a concept that will save you in any kind of relationship, whether it be business or personal. Legal disputes occur when expectations aren't met or aren't spelled out, so how do we fix this? *Upfront contracts* - written *and* verbal. Upfront contracts will save you in business and in your personal life. It's a simple concept but one we skip over so easily. You must spell out terms upfront with the people you do business with and very clearly set out expectations. I'm going to do A, you're going to pay me B by C date (don't forget that date!).

My friend had a great idea and ran with it. This deal eventually fell through, as Netflix lost interest, but had it NOT fallen through, he would've been cut out of a huge paycheck. And let's be honest, if anyone is granting access to their network like he was, he should definitely be paid. When I asked him how he was getting paid, he looked at me like a deer in headlights—not good!

How do we fix this situation? If he approached Netflix about getting a cut of this deal, they'd probably tell him to go pound sand because he's a small fish and not attached to any major agency. I would try that angle first but expect them to decline. You could threaten to walk and take away the famous pop singer/spiritual advisor, but Netflix has so many offers for ideas, that they probably wouldn't care. I wouldn't go with that angle.

A stronger position would be to talk to the respective teams of the pop singer and the spiritual advisor. You could frame it by saying, "I'm creating this opportunity to tell a great story on a major platform and show you both in a positive light. This is a huge opportunity. To get this kind of positive publicity through a PR agency would easily cost tens of thousands of dollars. Because we're using my contacts at Netflix, I'm going to ask for a 10% agent/broker fee, which is standard in most brokering situations." That is a very reasonable proposal, and he is pitching it to two guys he already has a close relationship with. The time to have this conversation is right BEFORE you introduce their teams to Netflix and right AFTER Netflix has expressed interest in this concept. That would be the peak of excitement for both teams. If they told him no deal, then fine, you walk away and they lose a great documentary over a small amount of money, relatively speaking, which would be unlikely. If they accept, then great, you draw up a contract and they sign.

When you are doing a connector deal, you are essentially selling access to your network. When you do this, YOU must be the one that communicates between both parties; do not connect them together until you have a contract in place! Very important. But aside from that, does your agent connect you with high level directors or producers? Of course not, they deal with the agent, and the agent makes that very clear to both parties. Ever tried going around your agent and reaching out directly to casting or producers? Yeah, you will get an earful from the agency. Same thing with connector deals; you have to be the point of contact otherwise you get cut out. But there is a huge payoff for it.

Another example of a connector deal is one I've done more recently, with a high-level director.
Said director needed funding for post-production for his feature film, so I went through my entire network to see if anyone would be interested in investing $50,000 for a movie. Sounds crazy, right? Well guess what, I got a few takers. That said, in this deal, I had everyone write down the exact

terms of how they would pay me. I did this in an email upfront, and later we signed contracts. That said, I would really recommend signing a contract upfront. I know many of you may be thinking, "I don't know two shits about contracts." The best thing I would recommend is to type up the exact agreement and, if you have a lawyer friend who is generous, have him or her convert it to contract form. There is a language that is standard, and a lawyer will add a few items that pertain to your state to make it a formal contract.

All of that said, connector deals can be REALLY lucrative if done right. Agents at ICM or CAA are not hurting financially. If you are involved in pitching a new documentary to Netflix or helping a movie get off the ground as a producer, there is big money in this kind of work. So much so that, after the successful launch of my first director client, I've started my own business finding money for directors and their scripts. Making movies is all about your network. Major producers make a handsome living off of it. I think this is a great way for actors and artists to leverage their respective networks to make a fantastic paycheck. At the end of this book, I've attached a contract template for your use that you can adjust for your own situation. This normally would cost thousands to write-up from a lawyer. You're welcome!

Other Key Types of Income to Understand
I heard a talk online recently which indicated that the three key types of revenue in the future will be e-commerce, social media, and real estate. Owning land has always been a money maker, and that's what we purchase once we get that big check or build multiple income streams. But in the near term, understanding e-commerce and social media is really important. Knowing how to build a large following on Instagram or Twitter is very useful for driving attention not only to your brand as an actor but to other products as well. This is a very important marketing tool.

A great example of an actor using his social media accounts and e-commerce well together is Sylvester Stallone. He built an entire merchandise site with T-shirts, mugs, etc. with all of his old famous quotes from Rocky and other movies on them. You may be thinking, "Oh, come on, that sounds cheesy." I guarantee you he's pulling at least $10,000 a month from that e-commerce site. That most definitely is not cheesy.

Another example of this type of business is subscription boxes. One of the most popular subscription boxes out there is called "Try The World." Each month, subscribers receive seven to ten sample gourmet snacks from around the world for a subscription fee of $29. You can curate your own subscription box as well by pulling together whatever you want! Curating products in a specific niche is key. This is a very profitable form of e-commerce that is accessible to anyone. Subbly or CrateJoy are great resources for creating your own subscription box to sell. I would definitely recommend investigating those sites as they are very profitable given the right combination of products.

Chapter 4 - Getting Down to Brass Tacks: The Process of Finding Your Own Income

Finding Your High-Dollar-Per-Hour Skill
If you're waiting tables right now, you're probably earning $1,000 a week. If you're reading this book, I'm guessing you're looking for a way out. I mean, I don't blame you; like every other actor, I've been a server as well. It's tiring work and bad on your body. Plus, you take the server mentality of being shat on into auditions, which is toxic.

How do we get you out of this rut? The first thing we need to do is take inventory of what you have at your disposal. And trust me, it's a lot more than you think. Pull out a piece of paper and write down everything you can do. I mean everything. This is what it'd look like for me:

Sales/negotiation
Airbnb expert
Car rental/Uber expert
Screenplay writer
Actor
Director
Movie Producer
Movie fundraising
Video editing
Voiceover actor
Website design
Non-fiction writer
Media relations/public relations
Business consultant
Resume writer
Commodities trader
Marketing manager
Cooking
Ballroom dance instructor

There are probably more, but my point is, if you look at that list, there are many skills that can garner a lot of money per hour. If you do a little research and go to salary.com, you can find out what each of these jobs makes per hour or per year. Here's what mine looks like:

Software sales/negotiation - $89,000/year
Airbnb expert/property manager - $70,000/year
Car rental/Uber expert - $60,000/year
Screenplay writer - $82,000/year
Actor - $68,000/year (that can't be right!)
Director - $75,000/year
Movie producer - $64,000/year
Movie fundraising - $103,000/year
Video editing - $45,000/year
Voiceover actor - $68,000/year
Website design - $86,000/year
Technical (non-fiction) writer - $82,000/year
Media relations/public relations $117,000/year
Business consultant - $122,000/year
Resume writer - $81,000/year
Commodities trader - $135,000/year
Marketing manager - $83,000/year
Sous chef - $56,000/year
Ballroom dance instructor - $65,000/year

If we look at this list, we pretty quickly get a good idea of where I should focus my energies for my side skill set based on dollars per hour made. Obviously, we all are trying to be an actor or artist full time, but that work will come and go over the years. If it solidly becomes full-time, that's great! However, we need a steady skill that can float us for the long haul. Looking at my skills, commodities trading (trading of oil, gas, gold, silver, foreign currencies, etc.) is the most lucrative on my list. I'm not living off of income made from this skill yet, but I practice daily because I know how lucrative it can become if one is good at it. And because I've freed myself from a 9-5 job or a 30-hour-a-week shitty side job, I've had time to focus on learning how to do this. This is also a skill I can do from home, or anywhere, from my laptop so long as I'm trading during the market's peak hours of business. You get bonus points for a skill that you can do remotely—e.g., trading, writing, social-media marketing, any kind of consulting via Skype, editing, voiceover, web design, programming/coding, etc. Being able to do your skill remotely is essential.

I think it should also be noted that as you read this, you probably already have a go-to skill that brings you money, aside from catering, serving, etc. We all have things we can do. As you create your own list, even if the highest earner isn't what you're most passionate about doing, that's okay. You may be a great technical writer, but have no desire to write as a freelancer. Or conversely, you may be a great nutritionist, but it's not the most high-paying. I think it's important to be passionate about what your side skill is as well. I have many friends that are not only actors and artists, but also nutritionists, life coaches, tutors, lawyers, etc. They love their side skill and make decent money from it freelancing in those respective fields. Passion is always key. I'll list my top five earners in order of what I'm most interested and passionate about:

1) Movie fundraising - $103,000/year
2) Commodities trader - $135,000/year
3) Business consultant - $122,000/year
4) Software sales/negotiation - $89,000/year
5) Media relations/public relations $117,000/year

Even though movie fundraising isn't quite the top yearly earner, it's what I'm most passionate about, with commodities trading coming in second. The other three I don't mind doing on occasion, but I'm focusing on fundraising for movies and commodities trading. You don't want to spread yourself too thin—it's always better to pick one or two things and focus on them as much as possible. You want to become a master in those skills. If you find that your favorite skill didn't make the top-five earning list, you should consider if it's worth doing for the long haul. That said, if you really want to do it, then do it. I think there are ways of making it work so long as it's scalable in a freelance model.

Maximizing Your Skill(s)
Let's say that you know how to build a social media audience on Instagram—I know a lot of actors are good with social media, so this should be a slam dunk for many of you. And I'm not just talking about posting pictures of you in your bikini and growing your audience. That doesn't count! If you have a real skill in growing a page's audience, the big question is, how do you get paying clients? I'm so glad you asked, and this is a process that is transferable to many skills.

So you're a whiz on Instagram and Twitter and know how to grow anyone's page or handle's audience—great! This is a really valuable skill.

Could you handle four pages a month and grow their audience? Of course you could. That would take you maybe 30-60 minutes a day of work. Guess what, you could easily charge a small business $1,500 per month to manage its social media and grow its audience. Let's say you wanted to specialize in dentist offices—it's important to develop a niche. You know how to do social media and you want to target dentist offices. I'm loving it. But how do you get clients? It's a lot easier than you think.

If you've never done sales, I know the idea of finding new clients makes your skin crawl. I started my career in public relations and worked for PR agencies my first 3 years out of college. The idea of sales made my stomach turn at that time. Ironically, I wasn't okay with making such a small salary, so I moved into sales and actually did well in it. That said, sales is just a numbers game and a process of taking your solution (social-media-marketer skill) and matching it with someone else's problem (need for social-media help). You don't have to strong-arm anyone, you don't have to bend anyone over the barrel to make a sale, you're just here to solve a problem.

I would start by compiling a list of local dentist offices—pull together 100 different dentists in the area. Rank them by most followers to least followers on their Instagram and Twitter accounts. If you're extroverted, call these offices up and see what they're doing currently for social media and marketing. Most likely they're not doing much. If you're introverted, I would recommend emailing each office, mentioning that they have X followers and that, if they had five or ten times more, they'd invest more into it and that you can help because you specialize in dentist offices (great news for them!) If you can get a conversation going or get to the decision maker, most likely the dentist, see if he or she would be willing to have you into a meeting. You're not trying to make a sale on the phone or over email, you're just getting that first meeting so you can explain your value. And from there you're just having a conversation about how you can help! I will discuss the sales process in more detail in later chapters.

Like I said, sales is a numbers game. If you send out 100 emails to dentist offices, you will most likely get about five meetings setup from people who want to hear more. One or two will sign on with you. Congrats, you just made $3,000 extra per month, and these are recurring clients. I swear, you can do this and you can apply this framework and system to most skills—social-media marketer, copywriter, nutritionist, life coach, etc. You want another two clients, make a new list of 100 dentist offices. Within a month of hard work you could be making $6,000 a month from clients on retainer, just from social media marketing to dentists.

I'll go through another example. Let's say you're a dancer and love dancing. Great. Your first impulse is probably to teach at a dance studio in New York or LA. NO. *Stop working for other people for minimal rates!* You would probably have a 30-hour-a-week job for maybe $25/hour. I trained as a ballroom dancer in high school and used to compete as a teenager. I was also a certified Arthur Murray instructor. After I received my certification 8 years ago, I taught engaged couples how to do a few routines for their wedding dance, *privately.* Do you see how specific that niche is? I became the guy that taught engaged couples their wedding-dance routine—have you ever heard of anyone else that does just that? Probably not. I was getting tons of referrals and charging around $75-$100 per hour.

But let's say I wasn't getting referrals, how do I increase my client base? You've gotta find engaged couples. Who knows engaged couples? Wedding planners, ring companies, basically any vendor that has anything to do with a wedding. What I would do is compile a list of 100 wedding planners and let them know that I specialize in teaching engaged couples a polished dance routine for their wedding. If I was a wedding planner and got this email from a dance instructor who had this specific niche, I would be delighted. Are you kidding? The planner could bundle your services into their entire package and offer a customized dance routine for the couple's wedding. That's a win-win for everyone. You would probably get five to ten positive responses from wedding planners—worst-case scenario—and have repeat business from those planners. Over the course of 6 months, each planner would probably refer three to six new clients, minimum. That's 18 to 60 newly engaged couples that need to learn how to dance for their wedding! Each couple would need a minimum of 5 hours of practice to learn their routine, at $100 per hour. You've just made $30,000 in 6 months on 5 to 10 hours a week of lessons—not bad. If you're a dancer, you know that teaching ballroom is a blast, so let's be honest, this won't even feel like work!

Growing up, I trained with a guy in Northern California named Stephen Nordquist, whom I still talk to 25 years later. If you grew up in Northern California, you've probably heard of him, as his ballroom dance business has been around for a million years and is widely popular. This guy had a great model. He wanted to teach ballroom dance to teenagers because he thought it was a great life skill. As someone who went through the 2-year program, not only did I learn how to be a wicked ballroom dancer at a young age, I learned confidence, which I was pretty low on at age 13, especially when it came to approaching the opposite sex. At Nordquist's, everyone rotated dance partners throughout the lesson, and there were seasonal dances throughout the year (i.e., Christmas dance, graduation dance in the spring, etc). The rule at the dances was that if someone asked you to dance, you had to say yes for one dance. Don't worry, no one was creepy. But it not only gave us a great skill, it gave us confidence, and good etiquette.

Why do I bring this up? Mr. Nordquist built an entire, AMAZING community of young dancers in Northern California and was also *very* profitable. I took the class for 2 years and then joined his studio as an instructor and his team as a competitor. At the time, Stephen brought in approximately $200 per student for a 16-week course. He had 200 students in his beginner class and about 125 in his advanced class. That's $65,000 over four months for two hours of teaching every Tuesday night at the Veteran's Center auditorium in Santa Rosa, California. And with the dance team, he paid us to help teach the classes (correct everyone's steps and posture, etc.) and received fees for sending us out to dance at retirement communities, etc. for the community's enjoyment. This is a guy that built a monster profit machine for fairly minimal capital investment. Not only that, we all had so much fun being a part of this community. It was a huge blessing to everyone involved.

If you combined a dance class like this for teens along with teaching engaged couples how to dance, you would be looking at easily a six-figure income on probably about 10-15 hours of work a week after you set it up. You could scale it up or down based on your schedule requirements any given month. You'd have total control and, guess what, you'd be doing what you love—dancing!

How Do I Find My Niche?
A lot of times businesses find their niche by accident. However, if you don't go into starting your freelance work with a defined plan, it can be a very rough 6 to 12 months initially, which is the timeframe in which entrepreneurs usually give up. I'm going to teach you a little trick on finding your niche that I learned in business school.

Using our previous example of dentists, if you're a social-media marketer and you're talking to prospective clients, the first thing they're going to ask you is, "What do you know about dentistry practices and how they pertain to social media?" Well, Mr. Prospective Dentist, I'm so glad you asked that. If your social-media marketing business has clients all over the place and in many different industries, it's not as strong of a sales proposition, which is why you need a niche. If you walk into the office and are able to say, "I know all about dentist offices, why they need social media, and here is my client list of *dentists*," it's going to be an easy conversation and sale. But how do we get this momentum rolling initially? If I'm going to target dentists, I better know anything and everything about how dentists market themselves. I would probably start with my own dentist and ask him if I could interview him about how he markets his business. You'd gain a lot of insights from that conversation about the challenges dentists face. Remember, you're here to help and use your unique skill to benefit others and their businesses.

So, let's say you talk to a dentist and find out that not all people that work on teeth are the same. There are family dentists, orthodontists, periodontists, prosthodontists, endodontists, and specialists in the industry. You probably had no idea about this (I didn't either!), but you're becoming an expert on dentists because it's going to bring you big money. You then would start a new research project on how each of these types of dentists market itself. Orthodontists are obviously targeting teens. Periodontists (gum issues) would probably focus on an older clientele. So as we know, Facebook would probably be a better medium for periodontists, given an older audience, and Instagram or Snapchat a better medium for teens, given they have a younger audience. I am not a social-media marketing expert nor do I know anything about dentists and how they market themselves, and I figured this out in 10 minutes of research. If you go into an orthodontist's office with a detailed social media plan of how to bump their followers and target teens, and you can speak to their exact target market, you are going to *impress* some orthodontists. And trust me, they have $1,500 a month to spend on social media.

In the method I was taught in school, using this example, you would draw out an X and Y axis on a white board and list the four most popular types of dentistry in each of the quadrants. So, top left we'd have family dentistry, top right we'd have orthodontics, bottom left periodontics and bottom right prosthodontics (oral prosthetics). See below for an initial diagram.

Family dentistry	Orthodontics
Periodontics	Prosthodontics

Within each quadrant you would create subcategories for sub genres of their businesses. For example, some orthodontists target teens, whereas others target people later in life who never had braces as teens. Those are two different market segments that advertise themselves differently. See below for another diagram as an example of this.

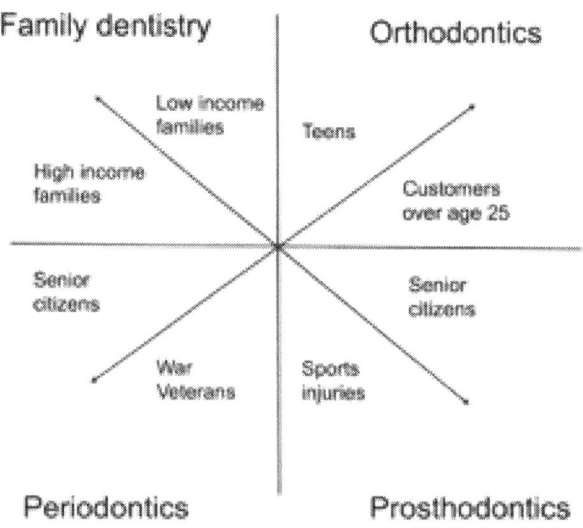

Once you map out the subcategories for each quadrant, start researching who does the marketing for each of these dentists with their respective sub categories. This may be hard to find, as many vendor-to-vendor relationships are not posted online, but they are sometimes. Many times on a site you may see, "All marketing inquiries can be sent to info@sagemedia.com/sagemarketing.com," or something like that. Or you can look at their Instagram page and see what's going on. If they have 100 followers, I'm gonna guess they don't have anyone working with them. In doing this exercise, you'll get a feel for who the big players are in your market when it comes to social-media marketing or marketing in general. This is important because you want to fill in the gaps where they aren't targeting business. Once you map out the four quadrants with the subcategories and see which agencies are targeting which quadrants and subcategories, you'll see where the holes are and know where to pounce for low-hanging fruit. This isn't rocket science; you could do all this research in a full day of work to get a clear picture of the dentistry market. If you're an actor, this is like preparing for a role—the more thorough you are, the more fruit this will bear.

Now that you see the holes in your market for social-media marketing, pick one or two subcategories and learn *everything* about them. Now you can really tailor your message, target dentistry practices with minimal Instagram or Twitter followers, and make a compelling sales pitch. Were you afraid about sales before? Trust me, armed with this info, you'll be snapping up new clients left and right. I don't care how awkward you are.

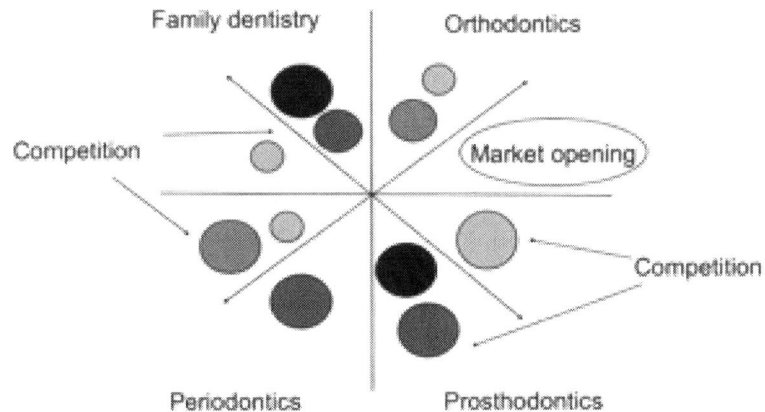

Finding The Pain
What does it mean to find the pain? This is Sales 101. Every business has pain. If I'm a dentist, I know *dentistry*. I most likely do not know much about social media. There are only so many hours in a day to learn. We only have so much bandwidth to devote in our lives to our main focus and passions, and if I'm a dentist, I'm managing many employees, keeping an eye on finances, learning regularly about new dental technologies, and going to conferences to stay on top of things. Social media just isn't a high priority, but I know that it's important because I know that all businesses need marketing. If you see a dental practice's Instagram page with minimal followers, you have found the pain.

Consider what I'm doing with this book. I can't tell you how many actors I've talked to who are suffering from poverty or hating their side job. And my response always is to them, "How are you going to live like this long term? Are you just going to give up acting?" The pain in this industry is screaming at me daily. So much so that I finally said, "Ok, I have to write this book." I'm not exploiting anyone; I'm literally just bringing my solution to your problem. I'm here to help.

There are lots of guys out there who talk about building businesses, startups, etc. Tim Ferriss, Grant Cardone, Robert Kiyosaki, and Tai Lopez are all great resources. These guys all have great insights into being an entrepreneur. One problem is, none of them have gone through the artistic lifestyle nor understand the journey of becoming an artist. I do. I've literally been fully immersed on both sides of the coin. We have a unique challenge in our industry to make an income on minimal time and capital investment because we ultimately want to focus on our artistic careers and have flexibility for auditions, filmmaking, creative endeavors, etc. Because I live in both worlds, I saw an opportunity to spell this out to artists like no has before. This kind of thinking is key when looking for an opportunity to build an income stream or any kind of business.

Building On Your Income, Passively
Now that you've got your key skill(s) down, you can build on that. If you set up four clients for your social-media marketing business, you'd be making $6,000 a month total on about three hours of work a week. Or let's say you set up a dance class every Tuesday night and also make about the same amount. Can you live off that? Probably, but let's keep building on even more passive income. As I mentioned earlier, you could Airbnb your spare bedroom and pay your rent. That's another $1,500

you've made—we're up to $7,500 a month on about 2 hours of work a week—that's $90,000 a year. Do you think you'd have time to audition or go to acting class with $90,000 a year coming in on 5 hours a week of work? I think so.

What if you tacked on a car to rent to an Uber driver to your income equation? You financed a Toyota Camry over 72 months (assuming you have good credit) with $500 down. You'd have a payment of about $350 a month with $125 a month insurance. You listed the car on Getaround or Hyrecar and specified that you're only looking for long-term drivers at approximately $60 per day for the rental. All drivers on their site go through rigorous background checks as well. You find one, and he or she becomes a regular driver for months on end in your car. This is paying you essentially about $1,200 a month *profit* (after car expenses are paid). You're just dropping off the car to the driver and they pay through the site. It's like Airbnb for cars. That takes your income up to $8,700 a month on maybe 5 hours a week of work. Congrats, you've crossed into six figures a year! And this doesn't even take into consideration your print, acting, or commercial income.

If you're really trying to get rich, you can scale all of these things to varying levels, hire assistants to run the day-to-day, and keep building new streams of income. I read recently that Warren Buffett has 92 different income streams—not bad! Granted, most of his are from dividends of investments. As artists, I recommend keeping our businesses on the smaller side, but still at a place where we're comfortable financially. Our parents' generation taught us that we need to have one job and one salary, but with the advent of the Internet, there is a bevy of ways for us to make income streams and scale them on relatively minimal time. The days of one job, one human trading their time for money will be over in the future. It is essential that you have multiple streams of income and, most importantly, that you have *time* to pursue your artistic passion, whether it be acting, writing, directing, painting, filmmaking, or anything else.

Chapter 5 - Not Just For A*sholes: How To Think Like An Entrepreneur

You may be reading this and think, "I would've never have thought to do some of these things. I don't know anything about sales. I've never been to business school. How do I identify when something is a good idea?" Let's talk about this, because I know this kind of thinking may be foreign. After all, you went to school to be an artist, not an entrepreneur.

How To Identify A Need In The Market
Remember before when I talked about finding the pain? That's all this is. Let's consider the story of how Uber was started. Their founder, Garrett Camp, was trying to get around Paris one winter night at the LeWeb technology conference and the taxis were a disaster. It took an hour or two to hail one. Because of this pain, Camp went on to create an app that would allow anyone who wanted to drive to pick up anyone who needed a ride—the slow taxi system was no longer needed. They had to adapt or perish. Garrett Camp saw a lackadaisical taxi industry that had no competition or need to pick up passengers in a timely fashion. Upon the advent of Uber and Lyft, taxi organizations around the world have had to drastically improve their customer service to even stay relevant—which is a great thing for consumers. I can remember the days in Washington, DC, when it took 45 minutes to hail a cab. Those days are long gone because of this technological advancement.

Don't Reinvent the Wheel
You may be reading this and think, "There's no way that I could come up with the next Uber app." That may be true! They went through multiple rounds of funding from high level venture capitalist companies. It was a huge undertaking for the company, and they've had a lot of challenges along the way even though they've been wildly profitable. Running Uber would definitely fall under the category of full-time entrepreneur and not fit into our ideal situation of "functional income."

MC Hammer once said, "In music, there are only so many keys on a piano—so many notes. Yet there is new and great music coming out all the time. The key difference in it all is how you market it." He's exactly right. Using our previous dentistry example, you know how to build a following on social media—lots of people can do that. But can lots of people be experts at building social-media followers for orthodontists who target a post-teenager clientele in Santa Monica, California? Absolutely not. You could count your competitors on one hand, *if that*, for that market. We're taking an established idea and tweaking it just a little to help it find its own niche.

Billy McFarland, the disgraced organizer of Fyre Festival, was promoting this festival with the ultimate goal of launching his new product, the Fyre app. The app allowed anyone to book celebrities for events for a very hefty fee. It was essentially the Uber of celebrity bookings. As we know, this entire project went up in flames in historic fashion, but I appreciate the way his entrepreneurial mind works. Do you see what he did there? If you're familiar with the story, he built an alliance with JA Rule, who had access to celebrities. Billy had a core competency of having access to many financiers (whom he massively defrauded). Core competency is a fancy business way of saying something you or your company is better at than everyone else. JA Rule had massive access to celebrities, and Billy could bring funding for the start-up. Billy and JA Rule planned to bring the celebrity world and financiers together, which created a combined mega core competency between the two of them. He didn't reinvent the wheel; he just created a combo platter that had never been made. The ultimate lesson to be learned from his story is that it doesn't matter how good of an entrepreneur you are, when you lack integrity, you can derail any amount of genius.

Thinking up an idea for yourself isn't rocket science. I'll show you an easy ideation process. Take any major brand or business model out there—for example: Uber, Netflix, Airbnb, Craigslist, etc.—and apply it to markets or demographics you're familiar with. So if I took Uber and applied it to actors or artists, what would that look like? Maybe you could develop an app where actors could order a headshot on demand. You pull out your app, order whatever headshots you need to your liking through the app, and a photographer in the area accepts the job. You drop by the studio, take the pic, and the photographer sends you the file and prints it out on the spot. You have a customized headshot or new look that you just took for your 4 pm audition. I just came up with that on the fly by essentially thinking of what "Uber of headshots for actors" would look like. One of you can go make that now!

I'll do this exercise again. What would Netflix for acting training look like? With so many e-learning resources on the web now, any acting teacher could record his or her classes, which most of them do anyway, load them online, and charge a subscription fee for beginners to watch. There actually is a website out there that is similar to this—can you think of it? Masterclass. Masterclass started with its first big online teaching seminar featuring Kevin Spacey. I wasn't that impressed with the content, that's neither here nor there. The point is that Masterclass has expanded to so many different skills and has masters teaching them. It's a great concept! You never have to reinvent the wheel—just take a model and apply it to a different market!

Use Your Own Pain And What You Know
In the case of Garrett Camp of Uber, he experienced firsthand the pain of hailing a taxi in Paris. This was his own personal pain. Because of his technology prowess, he quickly envisioned an app that could solve this problem. In my case, I got the idea to write this book because it was a hybrid of everything I've trained to do—start-ups and acting. Aside from that, I am constantly having the conversation with actors of what to do for a side job.

As someone who has started around ten businesses in my lifetime, take it from me, it's much easier to start a functional income stream in a space or industry that you know than in something you don't—I've done both. If you're a dancer, you know all about dancing. No one is going to question your knowledge about ballet or whatever you know. In my case it is ballroom dance. I trained for years and I'm sure you did too. So when you're building a functional income stream around dance, a lot of this is going to be a no-brainer. You just need clients. If you're a dancer and you're starting an income stream revolving around software development, I think it's safe to say you're going to be jumping into deep waters with a steep learning curve. And conversely, the same would be true if a software developer wanted to start a dance company. We all have our own core competencies.

When I started my car rental company, guess what—I didn't know shit about car rentals! That said, I did know a lot about Uber drivers, who were my target clientele, so I knew how to speak their language. I used to be an Uber driver in New York City myself so they also weren't able to bullshit me about prices. I knew there was huge demand for this market, however. How? Let me tell you a story. When I first got my TLC license (Taxi and Limousine Commission—all taxi and Uber drivers in NYC must have this), Uber had a partnership with a rental company in Long Island

City. I went over to this rental company and the lines were out the door to get rentals. I'm not kidding. I waited five hours to get a car rental—FIVE HOURS. Cash signs were bouncing around in my entrepreneurial head. I talked to a few of the guys in line—also new drivers—and I said to them, "Why are you renting? Why not just finance your own car?" One gentleman's response was insightful. He said, "I'm new to the city and country. I have no credit and I need a way to provide for my wife and kids. They cover all repairs and I just have to drive." I suddenly got it. I had never been in a situation where I had no credit and wasn't able to finance a car—it was my own blind spot based on my experience with car buying. I knew this was a huge opportunity because the lines were insane, mainly with drivers with similar stories. The opportunity I saw was essentially trading my good credit (selling access to an asset) and acquiring cars to allow drivers with no credit to drive said cars—a win-win for both parties.

When I looked into the laws and regulations of starting a rental company within the five boroughs of New York City, it was a hot mess. The regulatory environment is brutal, and you ultimately have to have an inside connection with the Taxi and Limousine Commission, which I didn't. This is true of doing business in most industries in New York City, by the way. It pays to be connected to City Hall, and it hurts if you're not. Just ask Airbnb. I wasn't trying to be a big player in the car rental market regionally, I merely wanted crumbs off the table of a multi-billion dollar industry. Crumbs would still be a huge surplus for me personally. If other companies discovered my existence, I have no doubt I'd be harassed by TLC and the departments of taxation, essentially putting me out of business. What was my solution? Run the same operation in New Jersey, just across the river. The Hudson River is a hard wall when it comes to the tentacles of the New York City government.

The first 6 months of my business were a bona fide dumpster fire. I had drivers in my cars with criminal backgrounds, I had big issues with insurance companies; it was a pretty big hot mess. That said, following these issues, I ran all drivers through an extensive background check from a private party after learning that Uber's background check was terrible. I also learned how insurance worked within the car rental industry. I took the "shoot first, ask questions later" approach to this business and, while it was a rough start, I knew it had a huge market. I knew that the rental companies in Long Island City were killing it, and for me, it turned very profitable by the end of the first year. I now have multiple cars rented for long-term contracts with drivers that have clean backgrounds and high integrity. A lot of people see my setup now and are really impressed, but if you were watching the show from the beginning, you would see the massive headache it was initially. If you're going to dive into an industry you don't know, you MUST research first!

Is My Idea A Good Idea?
Sometimes you don't have to test an idea to see if it's a good idea. In my case of being at the rental car company in Long Island City, I could see there was unbelievable demand for rental cars to Uber drivers that didn't require credit checks. When you see this kind of thing, you know it's a slam dunk. Aside from that, when I listed a car online for rental, I receive five to ten messages in a day. It was and still is a dog pile for cars that Uber drivers need.

That said, there are many ways to test your idea online. Pay-per-click with Google Adwords is a really great way to do what is called "micro-testing". Essentially, you set up a dummy ad selling a hypothetical product or service, and you can test how potential customers would search, what features they'd like to see in your product or service launch, and which marketing tactics would be most effective. Overall, you'll see if this idea is worth pursuing or not. There are a lot of resources online about micro-testing of product or service ideas, which I would recommend reading about so that you can test different ideas as you come up with them.

The Levels of Scaling
Much of the focus of this book is building *functional income* streams— keeping you afloat comfortably while you pursue your artistic passions and career. But I want to show you that you have options. If you think you can scale one of your functional income streams to double the income on a minimal amount more of time, do it! For example, if you have one Airbnb apartment set up, it would be a minimal time increase each week to manage another one once it was set up. That would double your income for maybe another hour or two a week. Is that worth it? Absolutely. We are valuing time first, but in that scenario, it doesn't hurt our time.

That said, let's talk about the levels of scaling, and I'll give you three tiers to think about as you approach any business idea or concept. This is essentially a way to scale profit margins. The three tiers are: businessperson, entrepreneur, and datapreneur. Let's discuss the difference between the three.

Businessperson
This is someone who is running a business, but the profit margin is small. Let's say you're buying lemons from a local farm and then converting them to jugs of lemonade and selling them to local lemonade stands. The businessperson is making a profit, but spending a lot of time for a relatively small margin. The manufacturing and farming industries have this problem. It's a lot of time spent for a relatively small margin of profit. This type of business or income stream isn't very different than working at a restaurant when it comes to making maximum money on minimal time. For what we're trying to accomplish, this is not what we want.

Entrepreneur
In the entrepreneur model, there is some level of scalability that is very good. If you're managing social media for orthodontists, much of the work is able to be scaled because of technology. You probably have all their social media posts planned out for months to come through Hootsuite, which is automated. It probably takes an hour a week tops to manage each client's social media because of how automated the work is through apps and software. This is our ideal model for maximum money made on minimum time using a high-dollar-per-hour skill set.

Datapreneur
The datapreneur model is the scaled version of the entrepreneur model. I have a friend in LA that at one point was running five Airbnb apartments in Santa Monica and making about $15,000 a month in profit. He was spending maybe fifteen hours a week managing that operation. That would be an excellent entrepreneur model of a business. But let's say later on in life we don't mind scaling back our artistic ambitions and genuinely want to grow our business. We are now valuing money more than time. What does that look like? This same guy later developed a company selling Airbnb market data to anyone and everyone that was in the industry. He packaged it for small scale hoteliers, larger hotel chains, and Wall Street analysts who wanted to see market trends for Airbnb and the hotel industry. Granted, this company is a full-time job for him, but he's a millionaire now. If you're going to work a full week, you might as well make it count!

Based on these three levels, as an artist or actor, we can see that the businessperson model is unacceptable for our needs, the entrepreneur model is ideal for maximizing money on minimal time, and the datapreneur model is ideal should we scale back our artistic ambitions later in life. Depending on where you are with what you want for your life, you can gauge if your idea for a functional income stream is acceptable or not based on these three levels of scalability.

Removing Yourself From the Machine
This is a very important concept because it is usually what stops businesses from scaling or what creates burnout for entrepreneurs. You must learn how to continue operations of your business or income stream without your constant monitoring should it grow big enough. Most of the time, businesses are built on the expertise of the founder or CEO. That's a great way to start, but we must develop systems as entrepreneurs to replicate our abilities and expertise. I've had this conversation many times with other friends who have successful businesses but can't grow because the business is tied to their own hours and expertise.

Think if Henry Ford had to build every Ford by himself. That would be a bummer for all of us, considering the automobile industry would never have taken off like it has in the last 100 years. Fortunately, he learned how to scale his business and remove himself from direct manufacturing. Later, Toyota developed the Kanban system to even better scale manufacturing of cars. This is a tricky thing for most entrepreneurs because they see their business as their own baby. Releasing control to someone else isn't easy! I completely understand.

Ever heard of Domenico DeMarco? You probably haven't unless you're a native New Yorker. He's the founder of DiFara pizza in Brooklyn, which annually is ranked as a top-three pizza joint in New York City. He is the opposite of Henry Ford. DeMarco refuses to let anyone else make his pies. Amazingly enough, he makes 100 to 150 pies a day as of 2019, at age 84 years old! While I certainly admire his painstaking adherence to the quality of his pies, can you imagine making 150 pizza pies a day at age 84? This is crazy! Even if you don't want to grow beyond one pizza shop, remove yourself from the machine! Dom has many family members to whom he could pass on his special recipe and process of making his world famous pies, and if he were consulting with me, I would recommend he do so.

Many times we fall into the mindset of thinking, "No one can replicate what I've been able to do in this business." I beg to differ. Entrepreneurs like Mark Zuckerberg, Jeff Bezos, and Elon Musk have many divisions within their companies that are fully managed by other people. They're simply overseeing operations and guiding the direction of the ship. Should you grow to a size within your business where you need help to manage or run certain operations, you have to train them fastidiously but then trust them to do the job. Releasing absolute control is a must, or you're going to be making 150 pizza pies a day until age 84—proverbially speaking. You're reading this book to free up time for yourself to pursue your artistic endeavors, not to become consumed by another job or business.

The Importance of Tenacity
What if I was a genie and told you at age 22, "The journey of an actor can be long and heartbreaking, but by age 30 you'll be on Broadway even though you'll go through 8 years of minimal work and insignificant credits." Would you take that deal? You probably would. I know I would. Eight years of frustration, but doing what I love, to finally hitting a big break at 30? No problem. Thirty is young in the grand scheme of things (even for actresses!). Artists, especially actors, have tenacity built into them. When I tell my friends who have nine-to-five jobs that actors go on job interviews two to ten times a week for a variety of roles, their heads spin. The nine-to-five folks go on a job interview about once every 2-5 years, and these are usually terrifying for most of the population. Actors go through an emotional meat grinder of rejection on overtime.

Why bring this up? Starting a business or functional income stream requires *much less* tenacity than making it in Hollywood or New York in the entertainment industry. But it does require some. Let's play the genie game again. What if I told you that if you devoted 5 to 10 hours a week for the next 6 to 12 months (if that much time), you would, with 95% certainty (following a well- thought-through plan), no longer need to wait tables or bartend or cater ever again. You would be able to set your own schedule 98% of the time on 5 hours of work a week, manage all income streams from your phone, and essentially be able to do whatever you wanted to do every day to progress your artistic career. Would you take that deal? Of course you would. Anyone would, but no one taught us how to think like this in school. The days of working from an office or being stuck in a restaurant are going to be a thing of the past in the next 20 to 40 years. It's time you learn to do this now.

Chapter 6 - What To Do With All Your Free Time Now? Career Gains

Let's say you took a 2-month break after reading the first five chapters of this book to setup your functional income streams using your high-dollar-per-hour skills as well as selling access to assets, and now you're sitting pretty with regards to your income. You're covering your bills easily and maybe saving $1-3K a month on 5-7 hours of work a week, which would be great. That is the ideal goal of functional income for an artist. Now you have A LOT of time to devote to your career as an actor, dancer, writer, singer, painter, filmmaker, etc. Let me spell this out for you how valuable it is that you've accomplished this.

I'm going to give you a tale of two actors that I know: one we'll call Susan, and the other we'll call Johnny. Johnny and Susan sat down together about 2 years ago and mapped out their escape from their respective shitty side jobs. Johnny was working 35 hours a week at a gym, and while he enjoyed it some, it was taking over his life. The company loved how well he taught classes there and wanted him to open other gyms around the country. While this may have been appetizing and lucrative, Johnny wants to be an actor first and foremost. He made the correct decision of turning that offer down, as it would've taken him away from his acting career goals. Eyes on the prize. Johnny had flexibility in this job to go audition, do the occasional meeting, or take off for a show for 4 weeks, but for the most part, he had to be at the gym. At this point in his career, Johnny had been done with his training for at least 5 years and was booking about two to three network TV gigs a year, with the occasional regional theater job as well.

Susan was nannying 30 hours a week and Airbnbing the second bedroom in her apartment. She was covering her expenses but didn't like the family she worked for, and they gave her trouble every now and then about leaving for auditions or any meeting that she needed to take. Her job wasn't entirely flexible, as she had kids to take care of with this family. Susan wasn't booking network TV yet but had booked a handful of high-profile independent films that were on HBO, Netflix, and Amazon Prime.

Susan took the lead on creating a plan to escape her nannying job. Johnny found it interesting but was skeptical. He wasn't sure he could make it out of his gym job. Susan felt that the plan was totally attainable with some hard work.

Since she understood how the Airbnb algorithm worked with regards to bookings, she wanted to expand beyond the one room she was currently renting in her apartment. She began approaching landlords locally who had listed a one-bedroom apartment and offered to manage the properties and split the revenue with the landlord. She explained to the landlords that she had a strong understanding of how the Airbnb algorithm works, which was a strong selling point to them. She didn't find these landlords overnight. She had probably 12 meetings with different landlords until she found two great fits. She knew not all landlords would be interested in this.

The first apartment she found came furnished, and the other didn't. She set up the furnished apartment first on Airbnb, and it was ready to go online almost instantly. She added a few minor touches to the place to make it more appealing for guests, e.g., added more cooking ware, a few decorations, flowers, etc. She had the apartment professionally photographed for a few hundred dollars and put it online. The first month she had about a 90% occupancy rate and made a $2,000 profit. The landlord covered his rent and she kept the remaining money. For the second apartment, she used the profit from the first month on the first apartment and bought furniture and also picked up a few items that were free from Craigslist (there are tons of things available there).

After having two Airbnbs set up, along with her own spare bedroom, Susan was making a little over $6,000 a month profit. She only had minor expenses to keep the apartments going, with cleaning ladies who had remote access to the apartments as well as laundry expenses. She also hired a part-time assistant for her properties to help with odd tasks. She was still nannying because she was running this entire operation from her phone. She later had access to an event space from a friend, which she listed on Splacer. She handled the bookings on that from her phone and split the revenue with her friend, bringing another $1,000 a month profit to her on minimal time. Her friend handled the actual guests at the venue. She finally quit her nannying job within 3 months.

After Susan had freed up about 25 hours a week for herself, she thought, "How do I use this time to maximize my acting career?" She began working as a freelance unit-production manager (UPM) for films. She was very well organized and began developing relationships with high-level directors. She pitched herself to directors as a UPM that could manage all details related to a film, like paperwork, SAG requirements, etc.—essentially a compliance manager for large scale films. Directors hate this kind of work because they want to direct, not deal with the bureaucracy of SAG or contracts. Basically, Susan said, "Bring me on your team, I'll handle all the nasty paperwork." She actually enjoyed it because she was working closely with semi-famous directors and very well-known actors. This was the trick, however—she had a retainer rate of $2,000 per month during pre-production and filming, but she gave a 15% discount to the director if she had a speaking role in the film. To save money in the budget, *of course* the directors agreed. Many times they'd let her pick the role because they knew how talented she was as an actress! Susan's freelance work as a UPM was technically "work," but she loved it, and it didn't feel like a chore at all. She developed fantastic relationships with very high-level directors and became an invaluable asset to many production teams. Aside from that, she got to act in very notable films with A and B-level actors! After many months of doing this work, high-level directors starting coming to her asking for her help. *Do you see the brilliance of what Susan created all within a year?*

Let's go back to Johnny. As I mentioned previously, Johnny was skeptical about this plan from the get go. His resistance got the better of him, and nothing changed for him. He's still doing the same thing, at the same gym, doing the occasional TV gig. Nothing has changed in his life. He's not anywhere near making the advancements that Susan has in terms of networking with high-level directors. He's solely relying on his agent for auditions and not making any headway of his own. Susan is getting more and more auditions now from her agents because she negotiated roles for herself in two major films with two notable directors. She is outworking her agent at this point on behalf of her own career, *which is what we all should be doing*. Her agent also has incredible respect for her because of how hard she's hustling on her own behalf. The auditions she gets from her agent she considers a "side salad" because she's driving the progress of her career now.

I hope you find this story inspiring because the majority of you are like Johnny and all of you need to become Susan. I became Susan in the past few years, and let me tell you, I can't even tell you how fulfilled I feel now. I'm truly living out my purpose now. You were never meant for your shitty side job. You need to develop the courage to get out because it is possible with hard work and a plan.

Compounding Progress For Years
A lot of stars in the movie industry have similar stories to Susan's. Many of them were stunt doubles for other stars previously (Burt Reynolds) or worked as a producer (Dwayne Johnson). Breaking through to becoming a regular, working actor has a lot to do with knowing the right people. Yes, your craft and your confidence/mind have to be in top order to book roles, but many of us have that in order. The X factor is who you know, not what you know. And that is true of every industry.

If we followed Susan's path compared to Johnny's path, how much more progress would we see over 2, 5, or 10 years for Susan? Susan is rapidly making progress by the month and meeting new and exciting directors as she gains every new client in her film-production work. Johnny may meet the occasional industry person at his gym, but it's not as direct as the way Susan would. The comparison of Johnny's versus Susan's path may hit close to home for you in an uncomfortable way. When I think of all the actors I know—and there a lot of them—most of them are following Johnny's path, and not surprisingly, most of them aren't making big breakthroughs in their careers. A mentor of mine once said, "If you're not out in front of your agent finding opportunities for your career, you're f*cked." He's 100% correct.

How Major Breakthroughs Happen
Whenever I consult with any company about their business or any individual about their specific problem, I love getting into the details with them. The devil is always in the details. That said, fixing a small business is way easier than fixing an actor's or artist's career. When a human is the product, it is a very complicated thing to correct. That said, it is most likely a problem in one of four buckets—your craft, your psychology, your type, or your network.

Only you and your acting coach or artistic mentor know where you are with regards to your craft. Only you and your therapist know where you are with regards to your psychology. Only you and your agent know how marketable your type is. But how do you gauge the health of your network? Chances are, you probably don't know enough people that can really make a difference in your career when it comes to your network. We need to change this.

If you've been in New York or LA for 5+ years, you've probably made a lot of great connections. That said, this all takes time. I've been in New York for almost 7 years and probably half the casting offices in New York haven't called me in yet. That's a glaring hole in my own networking, which I'm working to fix. But how can we fix this problem in an intentional way?

Let's first make a list of all the casting directors in New York as an example. I would then organize this list into three categories: casting offices you've auditioned for multiple times, casting offices you've been in once, and casting offices you've never been in. Now we have a list of who likes us, who barely knows about us or doesn't like our work, and who doesn't know about us.

Now keep in mind, a lot of whether or not you get seen by a casting office has to do with your agent's relationship with the casting office. I'm fully aware of this. In fact, I think this is actually the determining factor of whether or not you get seen by a casting office. However, if the casting director knows your work outside of the agent, will they call you in? Absolutely. I can think of about five different casting directors I've met through casting workshops, Actor's Access submissions, or some other way where we met—they liked my work and they call me in on occasion. That is a bond that was created outside of the agent relationship, which is great.

The goal of our list is to move all casting directors to where they know and love our work. An easy way to address this is to have a conversation with your agent about the offices that have called you in once and find out why they're not calling you in again. It could be a variety of reasons, but the benefit of doing this is that you're letting your agent know you are getting in the weeds with him or her on the details of your career. Usually, your agent will respond with a submission report and send you a long spreadsheet of a history of submissions. You'll probably see that he or she is submitting you to those offices, but they're not calling you in. So if they're not calling you, why not? There's a good chance your headshots don't match the roles they're casting. You may need to adjust that. Or they've just never heard of you, which you can fix with a mailing of a headshot and resume or by attending a casting workshop. You can also find out where industry people hang out, like film screenings, etc. I've seen a handful of casting directors at those events before.

As you can see, there are many ways we can push the middle tier of casting directors towards the place where they know and love our work. You may be reading this and thinking, "There's no way I could have that conversation with my agent. They don't like talking to actors." If that is how your relationship is right now with your agent or manager, get rid of him or her. I've been in partnerships like this earlier in my career, and it's like being in an abusive relationship. There are plenty of agents and managers out there who are willing to collaborate with their *clients—you are their client.*

With regards to the list of casting directors who have never called in you in, that's also a conversation with your agent that you can have and strategize together on how to get in front of these directors. There are a variety of ways to get on their radar as well—mailings, casting workshops, socializing at industry events, etc.

With filmmakers, we would essentially employ the same tactics, but I would recommend making a list of filmmakers whose work you *really* love. For me, I would *love* to be in a Christopher Nolan, Paolo Sorrentino, Martin Scorsese, and/or Quentin Tarantino film. When you are targeting filmmakers whose work you love, you're not doing so for the sake of getting a big break in your career, you're targeting them because you are operating on the same artistic bandwidth as them and you feel you can contribute to their own artistic vision. We are here to collaborate. That's an important delineation. Let's say, hypothetically, I met Marty Scorsese and I had the mindset of, "I would love to contribute to your artistic vision because I understand it backwards and forwards" versus "Please, please, please give me a role." I can promise I'd make a much better impression on him the first time meeting. The latter mindset comes from a place of desperation, and no one is drawn to that. With Marty, I'd be very curious to hear about his history with the Catholic church because I know that has been a large part of his life. It's even reflected in a few of his films (e.g., Silence). If I had a conversation about his experiences within the Catholic church and compared it to my own experiences, I guarantee we would make a great connection. Notice, I never brought up that I'm an actor. He would find that out later, incidentally.

This mentality applies to any form of artistry. If you're a musician or painter or photographer, any time you collaborate with another organization, you want to be on the same page with regard to artistic visions. This may sound like a no-brainer, but unfortunately, a lot of artists don't know this for themselves. If you don't know what your artistic philosophy is and what kind of work you want to do, I recommend you figure it out right away because the industry will throw you into trash projects otherwise. Always have a vision for where you want to go.

If we are focusing on building relationships with casting directors, agents, filmmakers, art directors, art galleries, or whoever else we want to collaborate with in an intentional way, I can guarantee we're going to make big gains in the years to come. Using our previous example, let's say Susan is using this technique as well. She is specifically targeting certain directors with whom she resonates artistically, but if she also can show them that she could provide value to a team by way of handling the nasty paperwork as well as being an actress, I guarantee the relationship will be a match made in heaven. The director very quickly will realize, "Wow, I really click with Susan on many levels, this business relationship really works." Ever heard the phrase, "Your vibe attracts your tribe"? Be intentional about your vibe—your artistic philosophy—and be intentional about attracting your tribe—the artists you want to collaborate with.

Chapter 7 - I Know You're Whining: Responding To Your Objections and Resistance

The reason I named this chapter about responding to your objections and resistance is because, at this point in the book, you're either feeling very energized or very anxious. If you're anxious, it's most likely resistance that you're feeling, because what I'm suggesting you do would actually change your life, but it would also be outside of your comfort zone. In Steven Pressfield's *The War of Art* and *Turning Pro,* he talks about how insidious resistance is to an artist. It holds many of us back from reaching our fullest potential artistically. What is resistance? Laziness, not wanting to leave our comfort zone, and not becoming the fullest expression of ourselves. We are constantly in battle when it comes to what we want to accomplish in our ideal selves versus what that lazy inner child would have us do. I'm sure you deal with resistance when it comes to preparing for anything artistically, I know I do. And guess what, resistance also holds you back from your fullest potential financially. You are most likely experiencing one of the following thoughts holding you back.

I Don't Have Any Money To Start A Business
I know you don't, which is why I'm suggesting the options I've outlined already. This book is designed for anyone that has minimal assets at their disposal. When you have a high-dollar-per-hour skill, you need minimal money to get set up. It's just dependent on your effort and hustle, which, if you are actor, I assume you have.

Additional ways to make money off of passive income, including Airbnb, event spaces, and/or renting cars (amongst other assets), also require minimal cash investment. You are essentially acting as someone who is finding users to rent out said assets on behalf of an owner if you aren't the owner. In all of these scenarios, you need minimal money to start your income streams.

But I Never Went To Business School
I assume you didn't go to business school as well. Through this book, I've given you some practical ways of how to think about business. I understand that some of you are very right-brained people with little business aptitude, and I've been trying to write for the artist whose mind is built like this. Some of us are idiot savant's in our own respective ways, and that can be a blessing and a curse. Many artists are like this.

That said, I think we need to become realistic about the changing landscape of the entertainment business. The days of waiting for your agent or manager to open doors for your career are a thing of the past. There are so many examples now of stars in the industry who have started their own production companies and are producing scripts that fit them perfectly. Since when did the industry ever serve up screenplays that fit us like a glove? It's pretty uncommon!

And let's be honest, if you're an actor, you understand marketing pretty well already. A lot of you are social media wizards, and when we talk about "your type" as an actor, all that is is marketing. Most artists have a good understanding of how art and commerce work together. A lot of this information is common sense but just needs to be applied to your own personal finances.

I Don't Want to Devote Any Attention to Anything Else Aside From Acting
I understand this sentiment, and I think it's fairly common amongst actors. I've heard this same argument from acting teachers, which I outlined earlier in this book. It's the ideology that "there can't be a Plan B." I respect that. But in my opinion, that's a 5-year plan, maybe 10-year plan, tops. You wait tables or cater for 5 to 10 years and you try your hand at cracking the industry in that time. The pressure of how much it sucks to live in poverty is supposed to motivate you to break through the industry. That would be a great theory if there was a direct correlation between your effort and career success, but there isn't. Why someone breaks through is a pretty complex formula that I'm not sure anyone could explain. Everyone's path is different. What I do know for sure is that, over time, the competition for your roles will continue to decrease. That is a fact that plays to your favor.

What I'm telling you to do is spend a lot of time for 6 months setting up your income streams, and then you can *really* focus on your career. If you're spending 30 hours a week bartending, I don't think that quite counts as "focusing" solely on your career. If we broke down your week as it stands, your acting career most likely is 4th or 5th in the ranking of what receives the most time spent. If we eliminate your shitty side job, we can devote *way* more time to your acting career, where you *actually* will devote major attention to it. A short-term sacrifice in focus will bring huge long-term gains in your creative career.

I Don't Have A Business/Entrepreneurial Mind
That may be true, but I'm not asking you to come up with the next Tesla. I'd be willing to bet you have the capability to run a small business. I have an actress friend who was in New York City all of her 20s working as a nanny, a waiter, and a personal assistant. She burned out on all three professions—I'm not surprised! She now runs one of the largest self-taping businesses in New York and has sustained herself in a very comfortable and profitable way. This girl had *zero* business training. She spent her 20s training to be an actor. She runs a business that fits her skill set of already being a trained actor well. Other actors become acting coaches of either classes or audition prep, which is a great way to use your skills.

That said, I'm just asking you to get three to four recurring clients for a high-dollar-per-hour skill and you're set. Or even add on an asset to sell access to beyond that. We're just shooting for functional income here but still giving you total flexibility in your schedule. When I have this conversation with people, what I find is that they actually do have the intelligence to run a small business, they're just fearful. And I get it, it does take courage. But as we know, your life in the restaurant/serving business is not sustainable. You simply will not last staying in that lifestyle.

I Don't Have A High-Dollar-Per-Hour Skill
Frankly, I find this impossible. There is a high likelihood that you have at least one of the most valuable, highest-dollar-per-hour skills in 2019, which include: project management, coding, copywriting, public speaking, search engine optimization, Facebook ad management, knowledge of Microsoft Excel, web development, app development, UX design, social-media marketing, and photoshop. I bet you probably can do one of these already, but let's say you can't. You can learn how to do one of these skills within a matter of weeks through online courses. There is so much information available online that it's crazy to not be able to sustain yourself through the Internet in 2019. If you signed up on Knowledge Society (www.knowledgesociety.com), it would give a wealth of things to learn that would all be high-dollar-per-hour skills. There are so many opportunities to educate yourself and convert this to a comfortable living on minimal time. It just requires your effort.

You may think after that, "Well, yeah, I can do one of these things, but so many people do those things in the market already." That's exactly right. Everyone does everything. And yet new businesses start every day and are extremely profitable—how does that happen? Marketing. You're not reinventing the wheel—you're putting a new twist on something that has already been done. All you need are a few crumbs off the table of a multi-million or billion dollar market and you will be living comfortably.

I Like The Stability Of Waiting Tables (Or An Office Job)
I fully understand that some of you may be feeling this as you read my book, and I don't have much to say to you other than this: if you truly are a person that loves stability, I would seriously reconsider your career choice as an actor, which is completely NOT stable. To me, that would be indicative of a larger issue, in that maybe you're not cut out for the artistic lifestyle? And look, that's okay! But it's better to be honest with yourself upfront. I know many, many people that like to have structure and do the same thing every day. That said, if you are drawn to be an actor or live

the artistic lifestyle, I would assume you *don't* like every day to be the same.

I Hate Sales/Finding New Clients

This is a real objection for many people and many businesses. We also touched on this earlier in the book in terms of how sales is a numbers game. That said, in some businesses, you're finding clients, like in the example of a social-media wizard's business of working with orthodontists. In other businesses, you're looking for consumers or customers, like in the example of the dance teacher's class or when you're selling a product. Like I said before, it is all a function of a targeted message reaching the right targeted individuals. If you want more clients/customers, you need to get your message in front of more eyeballs. That said, let's say you're trying to get four new clients for your social-media marketing business. I'll take you through some basic call scripts.

Rule #1 of talking to prospective customers is that we're never aiming to make any kind of sale the first, or second, or maybe even the third time talking to said prospect. The first time you talk to them it's all about convincing them to learn more about what you do. That's not scary right? Let's say it goes like this:

ALEX: Hi, John Prospect, this is Alex Witherow. I'm following up on the email I sent you the other day regarding your social-media presence online. Did you get a chance to look at it?

PROSPECT: I read some of it. We haven't really given much thought to social media. I don't see how it would really help an orthodontist practice.

ALEX: Right, I totally get it. Most businesses don't know much about social media and many people think it's just for teenagers, but correct me if I'm wrong, the more people that know about your business, the more people will use your services, right?

PROSPECT: Sure.

ALEX: Social media is a very organic way of creating awareness for your business, and it doesn't cost an arm and a leg like traditional forms of advertising. I know a lot of this may be vague or nebulous to you at this point, but what I'd love to do is setup a brief, 30-minute meeting with you in the next week to go over how other orthodontists are using social media and the results they're getting. Would that work for you?

PROSPECT: I'm pretty busy this week.

ALEX: No problem, I understand. How about a 15-minute meeting in the next week and I'll go over a very high-level overview of how other orthodontists have increased their sales through social media. If you're not interested after that, that's fine. At the least, it's just 15 minutes to learn what your potential marketing options are.

PROSPECT: Ok, fine, talk to my receptionist to set it up.

ALEX: I look forward to it. Thank you.

See what I did there? I just threw out a little hook to get him interested. I positioned it like he is missing out on the fact that other orthodontists are using social media and growing their businesses (which they are). No business owner wants to feel like they're not knowledgeable about some part of their business, especially marketing! Aside from that, I just pushed for a meeting, nothing else. This is key! You just want that first meeting, even if for 15 minutes.

I know the idea of meeting with a prospective client to sell him on your social media wizardry may terrify you, but think of it like this. If you're reading this book, I assume you're an actor, singer, dancer, or some related artist. Do you believe that it's important to go through training to improve in your craft? Of course you do. Has there ever been a Rockette that winged her audition and made the squad? Absolutely not. Those girls have trained for years upon years. If you're singing at the Met, you've been practicing singing for a lifetime. If you're on Broadway, they didn't pluck you off the street just because you look good. Trust me, those actors have shed blood, sweat, and tears at conservatories. What if you and I were out at a bar, could you sell me on the importance of training for a performer? Of course you could. And you would be very convincing, I would be willing to bet. So you see, you *can* sell, you just have to believe in what you're selling. As they say at all sales jobs, the first sale you have to make is yourself.

That said, if you're already a wizard at social media, I'm pretty sure you're confident you could show an orthodontist how you would grow his or her social-media presence. You know the formula. But aside from that, you have to show how it's going to increase his or her sales. All sales come back to showing how things affect the bottom line. If you go in there talking about how you have 150K followers on your own account, the orthodontist literally will not care. Everything that comes out of your mouth in a sales meeting has to come back to how your expertise will increase the customer's bottom line of sales and justify the $1,500-$2,000 a month that you're charging.

Let's say you're starting dance classes, from our previous example. In this model, you're looking to acquire more customers at a lower rate of pay as opposed to the social-media marketing company, which is taking a few customers at a much higher rate of pay. In this model, you really need eyeballs to see your message about your company. Once you have figured out how to market your company, again, this is still simple math. For every X amount of eyeballs that see your ad, 5-10% will sign up. Until the momentum really builds by word of mouth, you will have to figure out a strategy of how to get your name out there.

In our previous example, we talked about a dance company that marketed itself to newly engaged couples who needed to learn a dance for their wedding. The obvious people to reach out to here are wedding planners. Wedding planners could bundle your dance lessons into their own package and mark it up. That said, you would need to get on the radar of many, many wedding planners to drive regular business. There are other services out there that are involved with planning weddings as well so you could certainly reach out to them.

Again, in this scenario, you want to work backwards. How many new students/customers do I want and how many eyeballs need to see my ads so that I get the right amount of customers given my 5-10% conversion rate? You can use partnerships like with wedding planners, online ads (pay per click), referral programs, etc. There are a ton of different ways to get your name out there.

The most important thing to remember when finding your own clients is that *sales is a numbers game.* Yes, you are going to reach out to a lot of people who are going to turn you down. Guess what? It's a lot like auditions! Except your success rate will be more around 25%--probably a lot higher than your booking rate for roles. You will go through rejections, but once your income stream is setup, it's pretty easy sailing from there.

I'm Not That Motivated/I Don't Have the Patience To Do This
I fully understand that this may be some of you reading, and well, my only response to this is that the pain of waiting tables has not reached a critical point yet. If you're reading this, you clearly don't see waiting tables as a long-term solution, but if you feel yourself fighting me as you read, maybe you're not ready to make the jump yet to working for yourself. Like I said, this may go back to the stability issue, and that may be the hold up for you currently. If you really want to stop waiting tables, you will do it. If you really want to free up 25 to 30 hours a week, you will make it happen. Your life will be what you want to make it. Anything is achievable with a thought out vision and detailed plan to achieve each step.

I Don't Know How Airbnb Works
There are some great resources out there that detail how Airbnb works. The e-book "The Airbnb Expert's Playbook: Secrets to Making Six-Figures as a Rentalpreneur" by Scott Shatford is a great resource. There is also a website called www.pricelabs.co that is very easy to use and sets pricing for you by night based on the supply and demand of rooms in the area. It's pretty hands off, which I like. Personally, I have a strong understanding of the SEO algorithm for Airbnb, which is a combination of your rating as a host as well as price drops. Whenever you drop your daily rate on your property by $10/night or more, they bump your listing to the top of the search results for guests. If you read the above resource and utilize these two above techniques, you will be successful with Airbnb. If you try to wing it without understanding how it works, you will probably break even on your properties and find that it's not worth the time. I strongly recommend understanding the Airbnb algorithm to maximize your profit, should you decide to do that. That said, it's not rocket science. It's a relatively easy way to make money.

Renting My Car To a Stranger??
Yeah, sounds crazy, right! This is just another phase of the sharing economy, like Airbnb, which ensures accountability through a strong review system. That said, with an apartment, the guest can't run off with your apartment like they can a car, and that's a reasonable concern. When you work with companies like HyreCar or GetAround, they have pretty sophisticated ways of tracking down your car should a driver disappear with it. It happened to me once, and the driver feared being reported to the police so they brought the car back. If the driver does get reported to the police, they will be pulled over within a matter of hours

because the license plate will be flagged to all officers driving around, and they're constantly scanning plates; the plates are also being scanned at toll booths. Running off with a rental car is about as dumb of a thing as you can possibly do. Ninety-nine percent of drivers are great and very friendly. They all go through extensive background checks on the site to make sure you're not getting criminals as drivers. This has been a very reliable source of income for me. Additionally, the technology that is installed in rental cars now has GPS tracking and can remotely disable a car for non-payment. It has become very safe like Airbnb.

I Don't Know If I Could Actually Do This
You can, trust me. Most artists I meet are very intelligent people, but they've been told their whole lives that they only have the capacity to be an artist. As I said before, I'm not asking you to invent the next Tesla, I'm giving you small ideas to create functional income in your life to get you out of the restaurant industry. You can build on them once you have a system in place. When you start building your income streams, yes, there will be learning curves. In my own life, I know the first 6 months of anything new that I try will be a rough ride. There will always be things you didn't anticipate, but you will learn and adapt very quickly. Once you get to the other side of that learning curve, it really is an amazing feeling. Freedom from a shitty side job is truly worth the initial work!

Chapter 8 - Thinking About Quitting the Artistic Lifestyle? What It's Like On the Other Side

I had a conversation once with an actor friend, and he said to me, "Man, I am so tired of being poor. Sometimes I think I should go into investment banking for a year or two, save up money and go back to acting." This is a guy that has been in the industry for a long time—almost 20 years. I'm sure we've all had a variation of this thought at some point; I know I have. Let's talk about this, because I have been on the other side. For the record, I get cast regularly as bankers, lawyers, finance bros, sales guys, etc. *because* I know this world so well. Many of you have never sniffed an office before except for temp work. Let's discuss what it's like.

The Good, Bad, and Ugly of Corporate Life
In New York, the finance bros/Patrick Bateman types are seemingly at the top of the food chain when it comes to salaries earned. That said, when you talk to investment bankers (aka I-bankers), especially in their first year or two of the work, they are stressed beyond belief. Yes, it is true they're making roughly $175,000 a year initially. And yes, they are also working 80 to 100 hours a week, so if you do the hourly breakdown, it's not too different than an average salary in New York as any corporate professional. That said, if you can survive the stress of the first 2 to 3 years, you will make more and more over time, albeit with continuing to work very long hours.

I used to work in public relations as well as software sales throughout my 20s. Let's talk about the shit show that the PR world is. Public relations is one of those jobs out of school that seems really sexy, and look, our world needs PR people. Any famous actor has a publicist. While I was decent at the job, it's a miserable existence. One of the accounts I worked on was a national restaurant brand that I can't mention in this book or I'd be sued, but I was in charge of the daily news briefings to the client. Literally every night in America, there would be a murder in the parking lot of one of these restaurants somewhere in the country. Another person on my team was the point person and handled crisis communications with the client, so around the clock, they were dealing with daily murders and how to spin it to the press. Every single day! The stress was immense! Anytime anyone on the team screwed up, someone got screamed at. It happened pretty regularly. And guess what—my salary at the time was a whopping $45,000 per year as a Senior Account Executive, and the Account Manager was probably making about $75,000 a year. PR salaries are historically very low. After taxes, I was making about $1,500 every two weeks. That's nothing compared to what we could generate as outlined earlier in this book, and I was working 40 to 45 hours a week with zero flexibility to leave during the day.

Surviving Corporate Culture
Every organization has its own culture based on the people in it. Many times the press loves to glorify tech start-ups where everyone comes to work in their flip flops and pounds away on their laptops while sitting in a giant bean bag. While it does sound pretty cool, these people are still working easily 40 hours a week, many times 60 to 80 hours a week. That said, thriving in the corporate world requires a whole lot of a*s kissing. As unfair as this is, your promotions really come from about 40% your performance and 60% how much your superiors like you and like the way you look. Corporate life is very much a popularity contest. So in reality, your salary increases are contingent mainly on things you can't control. And if you get assigned a bad territory (if working in sales), you'll have a hard time controlling that too but still get yelled at regularly to pick up your performance (despite your manager knowing your territory sucks). And let's say you jump all these hoops—I've done it a few times—and you get that hard-earned raise. You're looking at a 5% increase, tops.

Every now and then when I tell non-actors at a dinner party or social event that I'm an actor, they'll ask me, "Do you ever get propositioned for sex in casting situations? You know, like the casting couch." I can't speak for LA, but in New York, this has NEVER happened to me. Granted, I'm a guy. That said, I've never heard of it here for all the actresses I know as well. I feel like casting in New York is very professional. Usually, when I get that question my response is, "No, that's never happened to me in the industry, but it happened some when I worked in software." People usually give me a puzzled look. When I worked in software, my partner and I were the gatekeepers to a large account, and we facilitated millions of dollars of sales, but we had to send all of our deals through resellers, according to government regulations. The reseller handled all the paperwork. So, my partner and I had to choose which reseller to work with. My sales organization was mainly full of guys in their late 20s to late 40s. Each one of us had to choose which reseller to send our deals through, and you guessed it, all the resellers were filled with hot women! I was regularly taken out for business dinners by total babes, and yes, one time, I was offered oral sex in exchange for pushing my team's deals through their company. I declined and, subsequently, that reseller spread a rumor about me to my team that I was terrible at my job, which permanently hurt my standing within the company. It's a dirty game in corporate America.

The corporate world is not a place where you can express yourself. You are a soldier or cog in a huge machine—questioning authority or any process is *not* encouraged. When a superior yells at you, you cannot respond or you risk losing your job. You have to eat your response. Trust me, it's not healthy. Do I think corporations are inherently bad? I don't. I think there's a place for them in the world, and they do employ many people. We all need our iPhones and laptops, right? Do I think they're a bad place for artists or entrepreneurs? Absolutely. If you have any inclination at all to be an artist or entrepreneur, corporate America is not for you. Blind allegiance and following protocol is what is required of you in most organizations, which is antithetical to the way an artist or entrepreneur thinks.

Why An Artist Would Hate the Corporate World
When I first started acting training, my teacher asked me in my first month of classes, "WHY ARE YOU SO EMOTIONALLY REPRESSED?" He literally had me write an essay on this topic. So I did. I went home and thought about it, and what I came up with was that after 8 years of eating shit in the corporate world and having to stuff down all those emotions, I didn't feel like I had the freedom to express myself—and I had a lot to express. Most of us come to acting because we have a lot to express. The art form itself is a great conduit for emotional catharsis.

Many actors go through Meisner training when they are young in their career. If you aren't familiar, Sandy Meisner developed a technique of getting in touch with what you're feeling in a split second and putting that into a line during a performance. His theory was that, as actors, we shouldn't give pre-planned line readings, only express what we feel in the moment based on what our scene partner is doing, thus giving a fresh and organic performance. This training is especially crucial for film and TV actors. When you go through a 2-year Meisner program, it completely changes your body and nervous system, whether you realize it or not. I definitely noticed the change after going through the training because I had *a lot* to unlearn from the corporate world. Before starting Meisner training, my body was stiff, afraid to express, and conditioned to fall in line and not speak what I felt. After a very hard 2 years of breaking these habits, I was newly organic and much more free-flowing as a performer. I also became much funnier because I could see the truth in any situation faster.

I know for myself that I could never go back to the corporate environment; my body and mind just wouldn't be able to go back to the rigid confines of being a cog in a corporate machine. The corporate world is about replicating results through rigid systems—that is the antithesis of an artist. I didn't like it before, and I definitely wouldn't like it now. I'm willing to bet you wouldn't either. You're just not wired for it. Even when you talk to creative directors at ad agencies—a job where coming up with fresh and organic ideas is a must—they easily get burned out because they are artists having to bow to their clients' whims. Like PR, the ad-agency world is also a tough place.

But You Make Good Money!
Let's go back to my actor friend's original argument—"I should spend 2 years in the corporate world, make a lot of money, then go back to acting." First of all, what makes you think you're going to make a lot of money in the corporate world right off the bat? Any entry level corporate job is going to be around $35,000 to $45,000. But let's say that, somehow, you scored an interview with Goldman Sachs for an investment banker position and you're ready to put in 80 hours a week for the next 2 years. The first thing they're going to ask you is, "So you've been acting for 10 years and now you want to be an I-banker? What makes you think you can do this job?" You may even have a 4-year business degree before you went into acting. They're going to think the same things I pointed out before—maybe not in as much detail as I pointed out—but they will be very suspicious if you can survive such a drastic change. You're going to smell like someone who is passionate about acting. And guess what, you are! So just own it.

In my last job in the corporate world, around 2011 in the DC area, I was making about $130,000 a year. That may sound like a lot, but it's not really. And during that time, I didn't have a life. I was being called by my boss at all hours of the day, and he was barking at me to complete this spreadsheet or prepare that Powerpoint deck. I remember thinking, "No amount of money is worth not having a life." I got severe anxiety anytime I got a text from my boss—which came at all hours. The more money you make in the corporate world, the more pressure and responsibility there is. I maxed out on pressure at the $130,000 mark. The nice dinners, apartment, and BMW weren't worth the anxiety in that lifestyle. I dumped it all shortly thereafter. Creating your own streams of income is the only way.

Chapter 9 - My Story As An Artist and Entrepreneur

In terms of my focus in life, I tend to vacillate between being an entrepreneur and an artist. At age 13, as I mentioned previously, I started in performance as a ballroom dancer in Northern California; for the 4 years of high school, I competed as well as helped teach dance classes. I also did theater some in high school. I didn't do a lot of dancing in college beyond anything recreational. In college, I studied at Baylor University (think Chip and Jo Gaines) and was an entrepreneurship and marketing double major. At the time, the entrepreneurship program was ranked #6 in the country. In my first class in the program, they threw us out into the waters of starting your own business. I literally was forced to start a business in spite of all my fears. I know how it feels to start something on your own—it is initially terrifying! I worked with two other classmates to start a company called "Jingle Bears Productions." (Baylor's mascot is the bear, thus the name.) We took talent from the music school and created radio/TV jingles for local companies. I had zero experience running a business, and within a year, as president of the company, I won 3rd prize for the Global Student Entrepreneur Award for the Southwest region of the U.S. We employed ten musicians, had seven local companies as accounts, and I heard our jingles on TV and the radio *all* the time in Waco, Texas. It truly was gratifying building a company that helped my school's musicians and gave a great advertising alternative to local companies that knew they were helping our students. How many hours a week was I spending on running this company while also having 15 units of class? Probably about five. (Are you noticing a pattern here?) The company was profitable almost instantly.

Upon graduating Baylor, I didn't really know what I wanted to do with my life. Acting didn't come until a little later for me. I spent my first 9 months out of college in London, working in advertising for the London Times. The first 3 years of my professional life, I worked in technology PR agencies in the Washington, DC, area, which, as I mentioned previously, I was not that crazy about. I thought it was way too much stress for way too little money. After that, I went into software sales and, at the same time, started doing musical theater in the area using my dancing skills and eventually moving into acting. I did pretty well in software sales for a while, and I was progressing in musical theater in the DC area as well. You may be wondering how a performer can have a 9-5 job while doing shows at night. In DC, you can do both, though it makes for a very long day. By the end of working 3 years in sales and doing musicals and plays at night, I wanted to try my hand in New York and start training at the William Esper studio. I quit my then sales job, sold my car, and went to New York City.

I did the summer full-time intensive at Esper Studio, and frankly, it kicked my butt. If you have ever done Meisner training, it's intense! I had never done any training as an actor, and to say the least, it was very challenging for me especially coming from the corporate world. I went back to DC for a year and a half and worked at a software company again, doing sales and going through a world-class sales training program. At that point, I thought I may have been done with acting, but I still had the bug. I finally moved back to New York City to pursue being an actor for real this time. With some money saved from my software sales days, I went back into training again and found a studio I really clicked with.

In my 7 years in New York, I've grown immensely as an artist and entrepreneur. I've trained with four different top-notch studios in that time and have run a variety of businesses. I won't go into my resume too much as an actor; you can find me on IMDB. But one of the most important things for me to accomplish in my time in New York has been to create a functional income because I know time is a valuable resource as an actor. Allowing myself maximum time to work on my career as an actor and entrepreneurial projects has been a top priority.

To be honest, I've tried a lot of different things while living in New York City. It is not an easy place to survive, and if you live here, you know that. Some of the "jobs" I've had include: real estate agent, Uber driver, reggae band manager (seriously), and Airbnb property manager, amongst a few other short-term gigs. Before Airbnbing of entire apartments was outlawed in Manhattan, I was supporting myself off of three different apartments. In those days, they were grossing in revenue $6,000 to $8,000 per month per property...not a bad profit after paying rent, and it took a few hours a week to manage. Once that was made illegal, I had to look to new options. I got an Airbnb apartment in New Jersey (different laws in another state) and started driving for Uber. It was at this point when I learned about the car rental business. Long in short, after acquiring four cars and putting four long-term Uber drivers in them, I've developed a very passive income.

Around the same time I got into the car rental business, I started another business, finding money for directors and their films. I started with a director friend who was looking for money for post-production on a feature film. I compiled a list of every high-net-worth person I knew along with other well-connected producers and raised a six-figure number for this director. Word had gotten around to different directors about what I accomplished, and guess what—I became friends with a lot of high-level directors pretty fast! I now have a fundraising company that works with different investors and producers to fund films. My director clients are BAFTA winners, Emmy nominated, on the director rosters of Warner Brothers and Sony, and making very high-level movies that have been successful in the festival circuits. In every project I take on, I negotiate a cash payment (typically six figures), ownership in the film via an equity stake (typically five figures), and a role to act in if there is something good for me in the script. Sound familiar? This is like Susan's previous story, which is about a friend I advised. She built a model for her acting career the way I did. Because I have access to funding for films, I have very strong leverage in obtaining roles, and I am working with the producers and director who are multiple levels above the casting director. Auditions for me now are a side salad. I mainly get roles through my director clients, and in really great projects!

Once my car rental business and Airbnb were smoothly running, I freed up a lot of time for myself, which I spent first on setting up my producer business. After that was moving along well, I started to learn commodity trading. I will say that this is a fantastic skill to have but a very hard one to learn. I've just started to move into a profitable place with trading, which will serve as another revenue stream, and I expect 2020 to be successful with this income stream. And lastly, I wrote this book during this time as well! The pattern I'm establishing here is that it takes a few months of hard work to set up an income stream, but once created, it takes minimal time to keep it going. Think of it like a plate that's spinning on a stick. Once you get it spinning, it spins away and you can set up a new one. This is the model I've used in my own life.

When you vigilantly value your time like I have, you refuse to take on a traditional job. After reading this chapter you may be thinking, "Wow, he has a ton going on. He probably works 70 hours a week!" Not at all. In a typical day, I wake up, I trade for two hours, I deal with Airbnb tasks on occasion (1 hour total a week), and I maybe field a call about one of my cars. The rest of the afternoon I work on whatever project I'm doing or on progressing my acting career. If I want to lay out at the pool or meet up with a friend one day, I can do that as well. Sometimes I have light days, sometimes I have multiple auditions or am filming. It always varies, but this is the vision I had for myself from long ago when I was sitting in a cube, mindlessly typing away, making someone else money. I knew I had to get out.

As I move forward the next 5 or 10 years, I see myself still acting, still producing films and expanding my fundraising business, still trading, probably phasing out the rental cars, keeping Airbnb but eventually doing it with my own properties, and hopefully writing another book! The key to all of this is to never stop learning. Once I get an income stream set up, I want to keep learning and take on a new high-dollar-per-hour income stream. When you free up time for yourself instead of working 30 to 40 hours a week, the world is your oyster. You can keep learning and setting up new income streams. My goal is to eventually have a seven-figure salary—and, of course, on 20-30 hours a week! It's attainable!

Chapter 10 - You Can Do This! My Final Benediction

I know this book has given you a lot to think about. I know a lot of these ideas will make you uncomfortable because it's very different than how you're currently living your life. Consider this: you already made the plunge to become an actor, singer, dancer, painter, writer, etc. That was the bravest step of all. If you can do that, you can make the adjustment to transition out of the restaurant world or whatever shitty side job you're currently doing. I will promise you this, however, your current lifestyle is not sustainable if you want to progress your creative career. And even if you took away your creative career, it's not sustainable for the long term as an adult either! So either way, you have to make a change!

Start Small, Baby Steps
I was 27 years old when I first heard about people making money through the Internet and managing online businesses from home. At that time in my life, I was making 50 cold calls a day and sitting in a cubicle. It took a few years after that to plot my escape from Shawshank, but I finally made it out. You can do the same thing, too. That said, it takes small steps.

Don't quit your shitty side job just yet. Focus first on setting up that first income stream. When you start to make a thousand a month extra, then work on scaling it to $2,000 a month. Then either grow that or start another income stream that can scale as well. As you diversify your incomes and start to scale them to $2,000 a month or more, you can start backing off your shitty side job. I think a safe rule is if you're able to pay your bills and save $1,000 to $3,000 a month after, you're ready to quit your side job. Be sure to *not* prematurely quit it. Putting yourself in a tight financial situation is not fun, especially if you live in a place like New York. You'll be home with mom and dad in no time, and that is definitely not what we want for your life.

All of that said, don't move too slowly either. If you really put your mind to what I've outlined in this book, you can find your way of the shitty side job within 3 months. A lot can change in 3 months with dedicated focus every day. It may seem daunting at first, but if you dedicate yourself each day and have a plan, it will happen.

Keep Trying Things!
I had a woman once ask me, "Do you have any advice for a young female entrepreneur?" This is what I told her: "Yes, keep trying things. You are going to be wrong many times, but don't dwell on it. The typical learning curve for any new small business is at least 6 months… expect to make mistakes and screw up your first 6 months as you learn a new landscape of a business. That's okay." She was very encouraged because I allowed room for her to make errors. Think about it, in baseball, if you get a base hit three out of every ten at-bats, you're a Hall of Famer. If you're booking three out of every ten auditions, you're probably famous! If you watched my day by day, you'd see some big mistakes that I've made. Sometimes I'm like a bull in a china shop with some of my businesses and have made some costly errors. But guess what, I keep moving forward, I keep adapting, and I always solve whatever problems I have—typically in a very creative way. I have enough confidence in my ability to think on the fly and come up with creative solutions that I don't feel the need to sit and analyze a market for months or years on end before actually making a move. They call this paralysis by analysis. This is deadly for entrepreneurs. Keep moving forward, keep trying things!

But Seriously, You Can Do This
An old acting teacher of mine had a very serious conversation with me about my emotional health about 6 years ago. He said, "You have very real emotional problems that need to be addressed. I have good news for you and bad news for you. The bad news is: you are the only one who can save yourself. And the good news is: you are the only one who can save yourself." This was a profound message to me because not only did I want to fix myself, he empowered me to take responsibility for my own actions and my own future. Six years later, I am nearly healed from everything we had discussed that day because I took the initiative to heal myself. Many of you have financial problems, and I have good news for you and bad news for you. You are your financial savior. There will be no bailout for your life or a savior coming to pay your bills. It's just you, but I believe in you. Some of you are living in a victim mentality—GET OUT! No one who is thriving in any kind of work is doing it through a victim mentality. You have to believe in yourself and know that you are the one who is going to bring yourself to a new place of success with a step-by-step plan.

You can find your way into a tight niche with a high-dollar-per-hour skill and build a lucrative clientele. You can maximize ways to make passive income. With the Internet and smart phones, so much is available to you now. You can learn virtually anything online. So many valuable skills are sitting out there waiting to be learned. You can run businesses from your phone. Seventy years ago, no one could start a business unless they had significant capital. They had to invest in product and have a relationship with a manufacturing plant. It was a huge undergoing to start a business, and nothing was guaranteed. You could fail and lose it all. Being an entrepreneur isn't for the faint of heart, but neither is being an artist. I believe you can master the financial side of your life the way you have your artistic side.

My Final Benediction
I wrote this book because I constantly hear actors struggling with their side-job situation and feeling broke. If I had a nickel for each actor I've heard complaining about lack of money, I'd have another income stream! I genuinely desire that you receive hope and a new vision for your life from this book. Where would we be artistically as a culture if Meryl Streep or Christian Bale or Quentin Tarantino or Martin Scorsese got stuck bartending until age 40, at which point they got tired of being poor and decided to give up on their dream of becoming an actor or filmmaker. Those actors and directors haven't always been giants of the industry. They found a way to break through, but they could've very easily gotten stuck like so many artists do. How badly do you want this all? Desperately wanting to be a full-time actor or artist isn't enough. You have to create a detailed plan of how to make it happen (hint: it doesn't involve just auditioning endlessly). Freeing up 30 hours a week from your shitty side job is the beginning, as you must learn how to network effectively; giving you examples of how Susan and I have done it is a start. Am I guaranteeing you massive success? No, we all know no one can do that in any artistic industry. However, 5 years from now one of two things will have happened.

In the first scenario, you will be experiencing moderate to massive success in your creative career because you've freed yourself from your shitty side job and have used that time effectively to meet the right people in the industry. Notice this has nothing to do with how many auditions you're getting. That becomes a side salad for you. You have to be the one to create opportunities for yourself and not rely solely on your agent.

In the second scenario, let's say you've decided to move on from your creative career for whatever reason, and I respect that. Sometimes life's circumstances change and we no longer feel like we need to pursue our artistic endeavors professionally, which is ok. In this situation, you've created a few functional income streams that were previously paying your bills, but you were prioritizing time over money because you wanted to devote that time to your creative career. Now you've moved to a place where you want to prioritize money. Because your functional income streams are scalable, you can continue to build them and proceed to double or triple your income by building them out and investing more time into their growth.

Either way, you win both scenarios 1 and 2. The only way you don't win is by working for someone else and building their wealth, while simultaneously choking off the time you need to devote to your creative career. It may seem scary, it may seem risky, but you can do it. Go out and build a creative and financial future than you can fully control and is also fulfilling. Godspeed.

For more information about starting your functional income streams or to learn about my consultations, please visit www.actorsstopwaitingtables.com.

Appendix - Sample Contract For Connector Deals

Please see below for the sample contract I had my lawyer draw up for movie fundraising or connector deals that I've done as I pointed out earlier in the book. Feel free to adjust to your particular situation. This will protect you when connecting others to your network!

Movie Fundraising Agreement
"Title of Project"

This Movie Fundraising Agreement is entered into and made effective as of [date] (the "Effective Date"), by and between Producer, [your name] ("**[your last name]**") doing business at [your business or home address], and [Title of who you're doing business with], [name of who you're doing business with] of [the name of their company], doing business at [their business address] ("**their company initials**"). Each of [your last name] and [company initials you're doing business with] may be referred to herein as a Party and collectively as the Parties.

WHEREAS, [company you're doing business with] intends to engage in fundraising related to the production of the feature film – "title of project" (the "**Film**");

WHEREAS, [your last name] wishes to provide, and [company you're doing business with] intends to accept, certain fundraising activities solely for the production of the Film; and

WHEREAS, the intended amount to fundraise by [your last name] for Film is [amount to fundraise] USD (US $X,XXX).

NOW THEREFORE, in consideration of the foregoing premises and the mutual promises and covenants contained in this Agreement, and other good and valuable consideration, the receipt and sufficiency of which are hereby acknowledged, the Parties agree as follows:

Terms and Commission Fees
The Parties agree that if [your last name] is used as an actor and performs the role of XX in the Film, he will collect and be entitled to a six percent (6%) commission fee on the total funds raised for the Film, up to $X,XXX. However, if for whatever reason [your last name] is not selected or used as [role] or edited

out of the Film, he will collect and be entitled to a ten percent (10%) commission fee on total funds raised for the Film, up to $X,XXX. For purposes of this Agreement, the six percent (6%) and ten percent (10%) commission fees, as stated above, shall be referred to herein as the "**Commission Fees**."

Minimum Threshold to Film
At the time of this Agreement, the Parties agree that the minimum threshold to film is X,XXX USD (US$X,XXX) (the "**Minimum Threshold**"). In the event [your last name] raises below the Minimum Threshold, and all raised funds have to be returned due to insufficient funding to produce the Film, [your last name] will not be entitled to receive a Commission Fees as set forth herein. Notwithstanding the foregoing, if [your client] [your client's company's initials] decides, subsequent to the effective date of this Agreement and with written notice to [your last name] of such decision, that it can produce the Film on less than the Minimum Threshold, [your last name] will receive and be entitled to collect the agreed upon Commission Fees herein. If any amounts fundraised are not used to produce the Film, for whatever reason, and are instead utilized by [your client's company's initials] for any other film, concept or script, [your last name] will receive and be entitled to collect a ten percent (10%) commission fee of what was fundraised, even if such amounts are below $X,XXX USD (US$X,XXX).

Costs of Fundraising
No amounts or expenses will be collected in advance of this Agreement and [your last name] agrees to pay all costs and expenses incurred by himself to accomplish and obtain the funding for the Film (i.e. airfare, travel expenses, etc.).

Surplus of Target Fundraising
In the event more than X,XXX USD (US$X,XXX) is obtained as a result of the direct fundraising efforts of [your last name], any additional surplus will be paid out to [your last name] in the form of an equity stake in the film. For example, if $X,XXX is raised, the original Commission Fee on $X,XXX would be paid to [your last name] and the additional compensation for the surplus amount of $X,XXX would be awarded to [your last name] in the form of an equity percentage stake. For avoidance of doubt, in the above example scenario, assuming [your last name] is acting in the Film (6% Commission Fee), he would receive a $X,XXX equity stake or a X.X% percentage stake in the Film. ($X,XXX/$X,XXX). Accordingly, [your last name] would be treated like an investor and be entitled to receive dividend payments like all other equity investors on the gross revenues from the Film based on their respective equity percentage stake of ownership.

Payment Deadline
The Parties agree that time is of the essence and that [your last name] will receive all earned Commission Fee, either by check or wire transfer to an account of [your last name]'s choosing, within thirty (30) days following the

transfer of any raised funds to the main bank account for the Film or by the time pre-production on the Film commences, whichever date shall occur earliest. If funds are used for another film, [your last name] will receive all earned Commission Fee by the time pre-production on the Film commences.

Nullification of Agreement
No producer, investor, or anyone associated with the Film team or [your client's company's initials] has the power or authority to nullify this Agreement between [your last name] and [your client's name].

IMDB Credit
[your last name] will receive a "Producer" credit on IMDB for services rendered.

Governing Law and Jurisdiction
THIS AGREEMENT SHALL BE CONSTRUED IN ACCORDANCE WITH THE LAWS OF THE STATE OF CALIFORNIA, WITHOUT REFERENCE TO ITS CONFLICT OF LAW PROVISIONS, AND THE OBLIGATIONS, RIGHTS AND REMEDIES OF THE PARTIES HEREUNDER SHALL BE DETERMINED IN ACCORDANCE WITH SUCH LAWS. EACH OF THE PARTIES TO THIS AGREEMENT HEREBY AGREES TO THE NON-EXCLUSIVE JURISDICTION OF THE UNITED STATES DISTRICT COURT FOR THE SOUTHERN DISTRICT OF NEW YORK AND ANY APPELLATE COURT HAVING JURISDICTION TO REVIEW THE JUDGMENT THEREOF. EACH OF THE PARTIES HEREBY WAIVES ANY OBJECTION BASED ON FORUM NON CONVENIENS AND ANY OBJECTION TO VENUE OF ANY ACTION INSTITUTED HEREUNDER IN ANY OF THE AFOREMENTIONED COURTS AND CONSENTS TO THE GRANTING OF SUCH LEGAL OR EQUITABLE RELIEF AS IS DEEMED APPROPRIATE BY SUCH COURT.

Entire Agreement
This Agreement constitutes the entire agreement of the Parties with respect to the subject matter contained herein, and supersedes all prior and contemporaneous understandings and agreements, whether written or oral, with respect to such subject matter.

Third Party Beneficiaries
This Agreement is binding upon and inures to the benefit of the Parties hereto and their respective heirs, successors and assigns, and no third party may seek to enforce, or shall benefit from, this Agreement.

Amendments
This Agreement, and each of the terms and provisions hereof, may only be amended, modified, waived, or supplemented by an agreement in writing signed by each Party.

Representations and Warranties
Each Party hereby represents and warrants to the other Party that:
- (a) It has the full right, power and authority to enter into this Agreement, to accept the terms contained herein and to perform its obligations hereunder;
- (b) The execution of this Agreement by the individual whose signature is set out at the end of this Agreement on behalf of such Party, and the delivery of this Agreement by such Party, have been duly authorized by all necessary action, including, as applicable, all corporate, member or partnership approval, on the part of such Party; and
- (c) This Agreement has been executed and delivered by such Party and (assuming due authorization, execution and delivery by the other Party hereto) constitutes the legal, valid and binding obligation of such Party, enforceable against such Party in accordance with its terms.

Severability
The provisions of this Agreement are to be considered as severable, and in the event any provision is held to be invalid or unenforceable, the Parties intend that the remaining provisions will remain in full force and effect.

Waiver
Failure by a Party to enforce or exercise any right in this Agreement will not be construed as a present or future waiver of such right.

Relationship of the Parties
[your last name] is an independent contractor, and this Agreement shall not be construed to create any association, partnership, joint venture, employee or agency relationship between [your last name] and [your client's company's initials] for any purpose. [your last name] has no authority (and shall not hold itself out as having authority) to bind [your client's company's initials] and shall not make any agreements or representations on [your client's company's initials]'s behalf without [your client's company's initials]'s prior written consent. Notwithstanding the foregoing, this paragraph shall not be interpreted to affect, impede or supersede any equity interest [your last name] may obtain in the Film in accordance with the terms herein.

Assignment
This Agreement may not be assigned by either Party without the other Party's express written consent. Any attempted assignment made without that consent shall be void.

Consequential Damages

Neither Party shall be liable to the other for indirect, incidental, consequential, exemplary, special, or punitive damages, including loss of profit or business interruptions, resulting from or arising out of, or in connection with, this Contract, regardless of negligence of fault.

IN WITNESS WHEREOF, the Parties have executed this Agreement as of the Effective Date.

[your client's company's initials]:   **[your last name]**:

_____
_____
By: [your client's name], [title]   By: [your full name],
Producer

Date: _____   Date:
_____

Made in the USA
San Bernardino, CA
26 November 2019